Dee and Don Inspiration

Dee and Don Inspiration

✦

Michael Pegler

FIRST EDITION

NGT PUBLISHING LIMITED

Dee and Don Inspiration
Published by
NGT Publishing Limited
1 Berry Street
Aberdeen
AB25 1HF

+44 (0)1224 841305
info@ngtpublishing.co.uk
www.ngtpublishing.co.uk

Copyright:
Main text © Michael Pegler 2007

Additional copyrights:
Copyrights for supplementary text and images are detailed at the end of the book.

All rights reserved. No part of this publication may be reproduced, stored
in a retrieval system or transmitted in any form or by any means, electronic,
mechanical, photocopying, recording or otherwise, without permission
of the copyright holder.

ISBN 978-0-9554293-0-9

Designed by John Brown, Design for Business

Acknowledgments

Many thanks to all those who have contributed so very much to this book. To Michael Pegler for his excellent and dedicated contribution; to Jill Todd for editing the main text; to the designer John Brown who has worked hard to turn the collection of words and images into a cohesive volume of work; to all the writers who have provided poems and short stories; to the artists and photographers who have contributed their images so willingly; and of course, as always, to Gillian for her never ending support.

NORMAN G THOMSON
EDITOR

Preface

A river affects more than the landscape it carves and symbolises more than the watery cycle of which it is a part. It impresses the shape of human experience for it stirs our consciousness, composes our vistas, informs our language and inspires our poetry. With these propositions in mind, the chapters that follow contain an analytic introduction and subsequent synthesis of poetry and images that are inspired by the rivers Dee and Don.

The first chapter will lead us to the notion of resurgence and other life cycles associated with the upper reaches of these rivers. This invites us to consider the historical course that runs through various aspects of the human journey. Accounts of Royal association, violent conflict and several instances of defensive architecture are described in Chapters 2 and 3.

Chapter 4 considers the many junctures that cross each river and feature in connecting ancient trails of human migration across this ancient landscape. The latter notion of many channels contributing to human association is transferred to the collective aspect of rivers, which must include the details of each catchment area, and so the fifth chapter explores the physical context and frequency of watercourses that feed the Dee and Don. This leads us to reflect, in Chapter 6, that other interdependent exchanges sustain the organisms of the natural world, such as those between predator and prey.

The events and landmarks of villages are considered in Chapter 7 and excursions through traditional narratives and folklore that emerge from earlier societies are explored in the eighth chapter. Sometimes places extend a notion of identity. They impress us by virtue of their unique character and the personal memories they entail. A place of such attraction and influence is presented in Chapter 9. The final chapter concerns the ancient Granite City and the convergence of these two rivers at a shoreline replete with wildlife and a modern harbour steeped in maritime history.

Contents

✦

1	Start of the journey	1
2	Kings and Queens	19
3	Battles and castles	37
4	Crossing rivers	53
5	Tributaries along the way	71
6	Hunting and the hunted	85
7	Villages and villagers	99
8	Tales and legends	119
9	A lowland hill	137
10	The journey ends	149

Chapter I

✦

Start of the journey

What establishes the start of a river? Rivers inspire us to consider the general concept of their journeys as analogous to other interdependent cycles of life. In conceiving of plants, animals, persons or cultures the young are ever identifiable as the offspring of some greater continuum where each end informs each new beginning.

Rising pools will spill into trickling threads of moisture then into bubbling burns. These young waters will fall in torrents and flow to join other tributaries in a single meandering course, emptying their freshness into salty estuarial seas only to return as rain or snow falling on sodden flushes where their young waters will rise again.

What we call the source of a river, where it rises, would indeed betoken a new start, the birth of new life. I see no reason to abandon this general convention in order to identify the start of our particular interests in this first chapter, although the notion that ends them in order to prepare the next phase of the journey threatens to be arbitrary. With the latter in mind, it is appropriate that I select the first juncture that will serve to embed further historical and cultural excursions. Therefore, the start of our journey coincides with that first phase of the Dee's course as it runs from the Cairngorms to Braemar, and of the Don's from the Ladder Hills to Bellabeg.

The River Dee starts its 85 mile journey from within The Cairngorm National Park. This is a predominantly mountainous place of unique aesthetic and scientific interest. It is the most recent and most extensive of British national parks consisting of 1500 square miles of land. Although people sparsely populate the area it is enriched by diverse and rare wildlife, including one quarter of Britain's vulnerable plants, birds and animals.

This environment may have once sustained the integrated life cycles of wolves, European bison, reindeer, arctic fox or beaver. Although this is not the case today there is a managed herd of reintroduced reindeer in the Cairngorms, and controlled examples of these other mammals in demarcated areas and highland reserves. Otherwise, a sample list of wildlife diversity that can be said to constitute a natural part of the environment in this region incorporates red deer, roe deer, pine marten, red squirrel, badger, water vole, water shrew, otter and the rare wildcat. Some examples of the bird life that may be found in the wild include crested tit, capercaillie, dotterel, osprey and golden eagle. The Scottish crossbill is found in certain areas, being the only singularly British bird. Although it is essentially a bird of the tundra, some rare snowy owl sightings have been recorded here and there have been attempts to encourage pairs to breed in the Western Islands of Scotland. A great variety of fish species abound in the waters, such as salmon, trout, the rare lamprey and, although scarce worldwide, there are expanding numbers of the freshwater pearl mussel. Finally, wildlife variation continues regarding specifications of tree, heather, moss, sedge or lichen, not to mention the vast realm of insects.

All the aforementioned examples of living journeys constitute adaptive responses to diverse topological variance presented by the land, its water and the pivotal influence of climatic and seasonal change. Ancient geological events and glacial movements have formed the Cairngorm Mountains and given rise to 52 peaks over 2900 feet in elevation. Ten per cent of the land mass now exists above 2500 feet, and 68 per cent above 1300 feet.

The Cairn Gorm translates from Scottish Gaelic as 'blue cairn' appearing as blue hills from Strathspey. However, the original name for these mountains was Am Monadh Ruadh or 'Red Hills'. Whatever name is preferred, this plateau comprises four of Scotland's five highest Munros: Ben Macdhui; The Cairn Gorm; Cairn Toul and Braeriach, the third highest summit in Britain.

The name Braeriach roughly translates from the Gaelic as 'the brindled upland'. It is here that the waters of the River Dee issue from beneath a mossy embankment known as the Wells of Dee, thereby constituting the highest location for the source of any major river in the British Isles, approximately 3900 feet above sea level. The Dee gathers its moisture into youthful water that runs ever faster, often through the frozen arches of late snow, until its deluge washes over the rocks of a sudden cliff edge before falling 500 feet into an immense corrie or cirque called the An Garbh Choire.

The corries are deep-sided hollows that sculpt the sides of mountains and valley headlands impressing with their structural aspect. Many accompany this lofty plateau; there are six to the north-west above Gleann Einich, and to the south, a further three. Glaciers carved the double hollow of the Garbh Choire lying north of Glas Maol summit. Its sides are precipitous, covered with scree impressively elevated from 2300 feet to beyond 3000 feet and from there growing into the contrasting form of the Glas Maol plateau. Garbh Choire lies close to Caenlochan and Glen Callater. Taken together, these dramatic compositions present a range of interests, valued from both a scientific and aesthetic rationale.

In Garbh Choire the substrate often presents schistose rock, composites of laminate structures that are both acidic and alkaline. The geology of southerly hollows reveals a category of rock altered by heat or pressure and hence classified as metamorphic. These mineral rich areas sustain diverse montane flora. Nationally and internationally valuable plants occur in the heath, grass and bog land found there, indeed some flowering plants and non-flowering mosses or liverworts are unknown elsewhere in the Eastern Highlands. In short, a complex structure exists, affected by variables in the geological substrate, elevation, gradient, shelter, moisture and the continuance of snow. This ecological tension of elaborate and disparate plant communities exists in a relatively small area that underwrites a special scientific interest. In what might appear a bleak landscape, in such harsh environments, the range of natural journeys presents a mind boggling spectacle.

There is vital conservation interest from within national and European contexts applicable to this place where sedge swamps occur on alkaline soils. As well as the nationally scarce sheathed sedge and russet sedges the latter sedge mires sustain dioecious sedge, yellow sedge, common butterwort and yellow-mountain saxifrage, and springs from the lingering snows also support other disparate mosses and starry saxifrage.

From the company of many interdependent life cycles of plant and geology in An Garbh Choire, the Dee then joins a tributary streaming from a series of lochans, diminutive lochs of The Pools of Dee, which travel with and sometimes within the mountain pass called the Lairig Ghru.

Occurring at the Pools of Dee as a narrow glacial channel between Braeriach and Ben Macdhui, the Lairig Ghru pass stands above many British summits at an elevation of 2700 feet. A large stone called Clach Nan Taillear, the tailors' stone, marks the area to which a story is attached, and retold in the fifth chapter of this book. We know that drovers, herding cattle between Deeside and Speyside used the Lairig Ghru, but Gaelic etymological authority is split regarding the meaning of the name. On the one hand the Scottish Gaelic for dark or gloomy is *ghrumach*, on the other there is a river nearby called the Druie, the root *dhru* (pronounced ghru) meaning flow. Many people go with the former rationale, the gloomy pass.

Ben Macdui translates as 'MacDuff's Hill' and has mysterious account concerning a grey man who walks this mountain, also related in chapter eight. Ben Macdui is situated in close proximity to Carn a' Mhaim, 'Hill of the Pass', and Derry Cairngorm, 'Derry' derived from Doire or 'thicket', collectively existing amid the Lairig Ghru and the Lairig An Laoigh passes. Apart from the northern side, Ben Macdui appears as a steep sided edifice capped by a domed profile. Northwards lies an extensive plateau to the Cairn Gorm. The ridge that links Carn a' Mhaim to Ben Macdui is narrow and long, dropping abruptly into Lairig Ghru on its western face. The southerly extent of Lairig Ghru is overlooked by Cairn Toul, 'Hill of the Barn', accompanied by Sgor an Lochain Uaine, 'The Angels Peak' and 'The Devil's Point', these three having distinctive pointed summits among a group of mountains distinguished in being plateau-topped. Braeriach, Cairn Toul and Sgor An Lochain Uaine incorporate the striking forms of An Garbh Choire. Potent topological events stir us here, such as the abrupt rise of a narrow ridge sweeping up from a small loch to the summit of the Sgor and, although of lower elevation, The Devil's Point also presents impressive fortifications on its southern and eastern faces.

The river journey continues as the Dee approaches a forceful descent of the Chest of Dee in turbulent steps that converge with the Geldie Burn at White Bridge. Farther downstream the rushing water is then pushed between a very tight gash, a rough incision of irregularly layered rock formations, after which the channel opens out into a series of circular pools, thereby constituting the Linn of Dee. A linn is a beautiful Scottish word describing a place where pools catch a fall of water, from the Gaelic *linne* and related to the Welsh word *llyn* meaning 'lake'. Allegedly the young poet, Byron, almost ended his journey here among the violent vortices of its currents. From here Lui Water and Quoich Water, with its own impressive linn, add to the river before Clunie Water and Callater Burn meet with the main course at Braemar.

Braemar claims the highest parish, golf course and highway in Britain; the latter being the Cairnwell, shared with Perthshire. Given its riches of mature trees and its serpentine river, the landscape around Braemar also abounds with a wealth of wildlife such as red deer, roe deer, red squirrel and brown hare. Capercaillie, black grouse, woodcock, siskin and the Scottish crossbill are sometimes sighted in these woodlands. Common sandpiper, dipper, grey wagtail and goosander are to be found along the riverside. Golden eagle, hen harrier, peregrine, buzzard, snow bunting and ptarmigan have been seen.

Famously, in September Braemar is home to the Braemar Highland Gathering and Highland Games, putatively established in the 11th century. The character of current games largely stems from 1816 at the formation of the Braemar Wright's Friendly Society, although older traditions persist. The athletics competition first occurred on the 23rd August, 1832. Displays of pipe bands and diverse hosts of fine tartan costumes take place at this Highland Gathering. Athletes engage in track events and exhausting hill runs. Characteristic field events take place including caber tossing, stone putting and hammer throwing as well as tug of war competition. One of the most exhilarating spectacles to be witnessed is the expertise and passion of Highland dancing. There is much to be said regarding royal history that grounds Braemar's story, but this is better related in subsequent chapters. At this point our attention turns to the emergence of the River Don.

At over 80 miles long and with a drainage basin of over 500 square miles, the River Don presents a distinct and equally significant watercourse. The Don is a different kind of river in many respects. Objectively, it has the potential to be just as inspiring and the land it frames just as evocative; subjectively of course, persons will tend towards unequivocal evaluations.

> **To people conditioned to counting wealth in good farming land, as well as in industrial potential, the Don is a river of far greater consequence than the Dee. Beauty is in the eye of the beholder, and I know many who will say that it is also the loveliest of the two rivers.**
>
> Graham, 1984

The river flows from the Ladder Hills to the Aberdeen basin winding through the communities of Alford, Kemnay, Inverurie, Kintore and Dyce. The Don's precise birthplace is located between Glen Avon and Cock Bridge, overlooking the ruined Delnadamph lodge. This embryonic Don comes into being as a confluence of several streams including the Feith Bhait, Meoir Veannaich and the Allt nan Aighean. Carn Mor is the highest of the Ladder Hills at 2600 feet. Its name is from the Gaelic, Monadh an Fharaidh, or 'hills of the ladder' and lies on the border between Moray and Aberdeenshire and South of Glen Livet. This place is best accessed by 'The Ladder' itself – a hill-path crossing east of the main peak. From the north, the approach is by minor road to Chapeltown of Glenlivet. A track runs past this place to Ladderfoot then fords the Ladder Burn at the start of the climb to the ridge. At the top of 'The Ladder', climbing to the cairn of Carn Mor is a gentle walk along an expansive ridge.

The Ladder Hills are also a site of special scientific interest. These undulating uplands surpass 2500 feet and constitute the most north-easterly of such altitudes in the United Kingdom. Biologically, the Ladder Hills are a good example of montane and submontane plant life. The area contains a gradation of plant variations from the lower heather moorland protected for grouse management and upper limits of the heather in the higher heaths and bogs. Important to this variation is the sequence of streams that lie between sheer gullies and a precipitous valley that cuts across the centre of the Ladder Hills. The latter environment contains disparate aspects and shelter for plant diversity.

The substrata of this area are metamorphic containing rocks from the Dalradian geological super-group. This contrasts with the more igneous substrata prevalent in the Grampian area. The soils that exist here become thinner at altitude, and are sampled as both acidic and peaty. The bog that covers this watershed is enriched with grey lichens of reindeer moss and hence, is designated as the most important place in Britain for this type of vegetation. There are large areas of submontane and montane dwarf shrub heaths and blanket bogs on the lower gradients of these hills. Traditional moorland maintenance sustain this plant community, although it is under threat nationally.

The degree of sheerness that a given slope presents forces a transition of plant communities according to changes in surface exposure. Hence, dry heather moor gives way to damp heath and then to plant communities more likely to endure remaining snow. There are a number of snow bed communities, especially blaeberry. There are varieties of plants that thrive on acidic soils and feed from ground water, as occurs in mire and grassland communities sustained by snow melting. This area has the greatest extent of rare blanket bog environments in the country, typified by the heather variety *calluna eriophorum*. The plant species that snow bed communities support includes: protected chickweed wintergreen; dwarf cornel; bog blaeberry and cloudberry. Sphagnum moss species occur in nutriment poor areas. Reindeer mosses are widespread in bog and summit communities as well as rare lichen, although lichen-rich vegetation is scarce in Britain.

The area also sustains moorland breeding bird communities including golden plover, dunlin and the rare dotterel. There are also raptors such as golden eagle, peregrine and merlin, which utilise this environment as significant feeding grounds. Large populations of grouse, mountain hare and other upland mammals may be found here. The mountain hare is sometimes referred to as the blue hare because of the general hue of its darker summer coat. Its winter coat is either almost or completely white. It is smaller than the brown hare with a rounder shape and shorter ears and legs. It lives up to ten years among heather moorland, rocky hilltops and, more uncommonly, in woodland as far as the snowline.

As the river flows for the first 20 miles through the parish of Strathdon, it follows an enclosed winding valley crossed by five large glens of the Deskry, Nochty, Carvie, Conrie and Ernan, along with other smaller contributory burns. The Lonach Hill distinguishes the formulation of the landscape significantly at this point where two prominent elevations protrude, affecting the river valley's course west of Inverernan, thereby distinguishing two sections. In the upper stretch between Lonach Hill and Cockbridge, tree plantation is scarce, but that is not so lower down where there is abundant woodland.

The hill tokens the Lonach Gathering celebrated at Bellabeg. The Lonach Highlanders march from Inverernan upon the fourth Saturday of August. The March of the Clansmen is realised in full Highland costume wielding pikes and a type of battleaxe called a Lochaber – an event to rival the traditions of Braemar. The men of Lonach parade the arena following the longer march before the homes of the gathering's local patronage. These Highland Games are supported by accomplished athletes, pipers and dancers, who compete in various competitions with good humour, enthusiasm and great skill.

As the rivers Dee and Don flow through and beyond Braemar and Bellebeg respectively, the physical evidence of complex human journeys proliferates and interweaves farther and deeper. Documented history, extant structures and the living traditions of people serve to focus the subsequent chapters of this book. Our next departure is an excursion through the chronicles of royalty.

POSTCARD

I am bathed in laughter, a music sparkling
Through the mist to echo in the corries,
From haughty ben to humble scree, past the Larig Ghru.
I fell from the edge of Mar in the Caledonian Forest,
Tumble on this granite bed of the rising ice-cold Dee;
A fruit of the pine, in water pure as heaven.

No more the wind sings through my scales as I drift on,
Regardless, crashing where the shadows stoop,
The verdant hum of flora. I prepare for cataracts, break
Into the bastion of the salmon; from kettledrums
To nettled drops, beyond the pasture's babble:
Rutting deer, a fox's bark, fleeting sheep and cattle.

Descent is ever east, to a royal feast of 'scenic',
Where shortbread tins have Lochnagar in trews,
Glinting lochs and ragamuffin skies. I feel a drop
Of litter, the land begin to change into a broad
And contoured view, paths and trails for lovers,
Find myself in the doldrums of a sliver.

A humpback bridge, concrete, bricks,
Till I'm kissing the lips of the suburbs – a wall
Of noise and a whiff of greed in the air,
A salty swell and the streets aweigh with traffic.
So here I am at Girdle Ness, a cold egress
To herring ghosts and the dream of hydrocarbons.

Douglas W Gray

MITHER DEE

Hotterin an oozin frae the Wells o Dee,
The river winds lang on her wey tae the sea.
Ower Braeriach's grim cliff, she loups tae the Glen,
Neath craggy, auld faces o' harsh mountain ben.

Bubblin an chatterin in grey-granite rills,
Swalled wi the peat-burns frae shelterin hills.
Doon at the Linn, roarin through the scoored gorge,
Syne spreadin her fingers afore bonny Mar Lodge.

She hoves doon the Valley frae Braemar tae the sea,
Past auld Scots pines and bonny green lea.
Through low-hingin laricks an fir-scented tang,
She gaithers her bairns, growin wider and strang.

The hert o the Valley, aye lo'ed by her ain,
The Dee cuts the land, like a life-bringin vein.
Fyles roarin in spate or flowin sae calm,
The soun o her waaters aye like a balm.
The fowk o The Glen are bit here for a fyle,
Bit eternal, auld Dee flows on mile upon mile,
Teemin her bounty intae the muckle saat sea,
Like a mither, aye faithful, this bonny-bit Dee.

MARY MUNRO

SOURCE

Far to the west
beyond the green fields
the woods
and the low lying hills

deep in the granite heart
a river is born

urgent

soft as a woman

BRIAN LAWRIE

DEE JOURNEY

A caller skelp o stane an storm,
Braeriach's sides are tempest-torn;
An in yon weety, derksome wame,
Whaur win is ice an sun's a flame,
The birlin Dee is born.
A sna-brig haps her growing tide,
Till, breengin up wi kittled pride,
She's heelstergowdie ower a crag!
A frichtsome drap – this watter-hag
Cowps doon a corrie's bride.
Three lochs, disjaskit, dreich as dule,
She lies neth blearie Cairn Toul,
Till, necklet o the Norlan bree
She's glintin ower the Chest o Dee
A jimp an jibblin jewel.
Syne reemin on intil the linn,
Whaur warrior crags rise sterk abune,
An at their foun, an in aneth
Wi feint the whisper on a braith
O win, aa's dreepin, deep as daith,
As seeister as sin.
Ayont the gallows tree o Mar
She's lowsed an liltin fur Braemar
An ilkie burn, on ilkie Ben,
Will jink its cloudy, Heilan den
Tae jine her near an far.
Wi widded hills at ilkie gait
An salmon slidderin doon the spate,
She wallops neth a winsome brig,
Her waves, wud meers afore a gig,
Lowp up in touslie fete.
Atap her faem the kelpies ride,
The deer an eaglet rin astride
Till, pitten on a hamely goun,
She weary-wins a muckle toun
An, fair ferfochen, settles doon
Tae coost her braws aside.

SHEENA BLACKHALL

THE STORM

near Invercauld

The river is a line of bucking plasma
in red light fantasie;

a swirl of limbs and loins
in once in a while debauch;

ecstatic disequilibrium
the storm about to break;

a wild ejaculation
spilled and sated on the land.

BRAIN LAWRIE

SPRING IN THE DEE VALLEY

Fare thee weel, deid, auld Winter.
We've tholed yer coorseness gey lang.
Haste ye back, yon bonny saft air
Fan the valley dirls wi sweet sang,
An Spring claithes the land aince cauld an bare.

Saft, mochy green loups frae the hard, broon grun.
A pale-yalla primrose keeks in a furl o leaves.
Fresh floories star the mossy, green braes,
An the bonny birks flutter their tasselly goons
As Nature welcomes the Spring's mild days.

Sna-bree sings doon ilka sma rill
As the corries gie up their blanket o fite,
An life flows again in the Land o the Hills
Far Winter sleeps lang, deep an still.
Bleed flows again in the veins o the land,
An my cauld hairt wi new hope fills.

Mary Munro

THE BONNIE BANKS O DEE

Tho springtime gars the sna-bree rin
An sweet's the day, wi blossom bricht,
Oh yatterin peesie haud yer wheesht,
For aa tae me is constant nicht.

Tho simmer turn the barley broon,
The sonsie heids I canna see,
For, thinkin on the braes o hame,
The brimming tearlicht blins the ee.

Oh Autumn, hap yer winsome face,
An dinna shine yer favours here,
Till my fit's firm upon the heath,
Aa's waesome, dreich an drear.

The Shiftin Seasons are as ain,
Cauld Winter iver follows me,
Fur Simmer is the ae dear place,
The bonnie banks of Dee.

SHEENA BLACKHALL

THE DEE

It shines like diamonds
All in a cavern
It roams the hills
To find the sea
The Dee

Josh Banks

The Cairngorms, birthplace of the Dee

BILL ANDERSON

Michael Pegler

Braeriach, Cairngorms

Andrew Scott-Martin

Chapter 2

Kings and Queens

The causal cycles of nature flow through the bloodlines of people. Through thousands of years of subsequent associations, people come to organise communities through bonds of loyalty to family, tribe and hierarchies of governance. From the eighth or ninth centuries the pulse of royal lineage has continued to provide a structure to the chronicles of human development in the land of the Dee and Don.

Doldencha, *Dail-dun-atha*, is Scots Gaelic for 'fort at the haugh ford'. Haugh is a Scots term for lowlands near streams or rivers that are prone to flooding. Doldencha, situated near the Braemar of today, was an eighth century fortification in the Celtic province of Mar. At that time chiefs, or *mormaers*, ruled each province. There were three other provinces in Aberdeenshire; Garioch, Buchan and Strathbogie. All had a regal lineage.

Kenneth MacAlpine, Kenneth II (971–995) was the son of Malcolm I and great-great-grandson of Kenneth I. This line continued through King Kenneth III (997–1005), the son of Duff and brother of Kenneth II, after whom came Malcolm II (1005–1034). Malcolm appears on Deeside, travelling north to meet a Danish invasion in 1010 and again in 1012. He died at Glamis, the last male descendent of the MacAlpine line, Kenneth I (843–858).

Duncan I (1034–1040) was the eldest son of Bethoc, the eldest daughter of Malcolm II, and Crinan, hereditary Abbot of Dunkeld. Thorfinn was the son of Donada, another daughter of Malcolm II, who was married to Sigurd, Jarl of Orkney. Malcolm's second daughter, Donda, was married to Finlac the Mormaer of Moravia (Moray). Their son was *Maelbetha* or MacBeth (1040–1057). These three grandsons of Malcolm II became enemies.

MacBeth, secretly in league with Thorfinn, fought alongside Duncan I against Thorfinn's forces on the Morayshire coast. Thorfinn pursued Duncan's army to Deeside, to a place that later betokens his name – Torphins. Duncan was wounded and MacBeth took him to a blacksmith's cottage to kill him, thereby effectively claiming kingship.

MacBeth's Queen was Gruoch. It is now thought that Gruoch was the daughter of Kenneth III's son, Boite, hence Kenneth III was Gruoch's grandfather, not Kenneth II as previously supposed. Gruoch's first marriage was to Gillecomgain, the nephew of MacBeth's father, Finlay the Mormaer of Moray. Gruoch's son from this first marriage was Lulach. It is said MacBeth claimed that his stepson, Lulach 'the fatuous', was the rightful heir, so MacBeth ruled in Lulach's stead and intended to remove all challenges. However, Duncan's sons escaped and the eldest, Malcolm, sought revenge.

There were several passes through 'The Mounth', the Grampian uplands, and MacBeth fled to Deeside by Cairn a' Mounth crossing the Dee at Kincardine o' Neil and on to the Peel of Lumphanan, pursued by Malcom and MacDuff. Malcolm rested at Kincardine o' Neil but MacDuff persisted, and slew MacBeth on the slopes of Perkhill, cutting off his head and presenting it to Malcolm. MacDuff also killed Lulach and thereby Malcolm gained accession to kingship.

Malcolm III (1057–1093) was Malcolm Canmore, *Ceann Mor*, or 'Great Head'. The reign of Malcolm III and his subsequent eight successors from 1057 to 1289 presided over extreme social changes. Malcolm first married Thorfinn's widow, Ingebjorg, who died in 1068. He then married Margaret Atheling, known as St Margaret of Scotland, who spent most of her time at Doldencha. As mentioned earlier, Malcolm was credited with starting the tradition of Braemar's Gathering of the Clans.

Queen Margaret was originally from Hungary. She was critical of certain practices of the Celtic Church and insisted upon publicly debating the issues of Lent, marriage practices and certain barbarous rites. She was intent upon rewarding good examples of spirituality, so visited hermits with offerings. Her gifts were refused, for the hermits had vowed to observe a life of poverty, so Margaret asked them to set her charitable tasks instead.

In 1093 Canmore attempted a fifth invasion of England and was killed at Alnwick, and his son, Edward, was fatally wounded. Queen Margaret died in Edinburgh Castle soon after hearing the news. Queen Margaret was canonised St Margaret in 1251 by Pope Innocent IV. The Episcopal Church of St Margaret is found in Braemar today.

The reign of Alexander I (1107–1124) – Alexander 'the fierce' – was eclipsed by his younger brother, David I (1124–1153). This reign eventually brought feudalism and introduced two chivalric orders, the Knights Templars and Knights Hospitallers, to Deeside.

David's 11-year-old grandson Malcolm IV (1153–1165) succeeded him, known as 'the maiden' because of his gentle appearance. In 1162 Malcolm IV travelled through Elsick Mounth into Deeside to socialise with Jarl Sewin Asleifsson, the last Viking King. It is said that *Apadion* or Aberdeen was the venue. Malcolm IV died in 1165, succeeded by his younger brother William 'the lion' (1165–1214).

William regularly journeyed to Deeside using Elsick Mounth, and built a palace in Aberdeen. Upon suppressing a Celtic rebellion in 1212 he led his powerful army through the Dee valley and across Cairn a' Mounth. William later appeared on Deeside with an entourage that included the De Beyseth family – the Bissets – whom the king established in Aboyne. In 1187 William gave the lands of Culter to the Knights Templars. From 1221 and 1236 Walter Bisset set up the Preceptory of Templars at Culter. Radulphus, Bishop of Aberdeen, later gave the Kirk of Formaston at Aboyne to this Preceptory, thereby securing this chivalric order in the valley.

William's son, Alexander II (1214–1249), was the next accession. By this time the Bissets' prestige and power had risen as indicated by their signature upon Royal Charters. Alexander II and his queen, Marie de Coucy, also frequented Aboyne, but their friendship with the Bissets caused jealousy and their eventual exile. Alexander II retained affection for Deeside and forfeited Aboyne to the Crown as a royal burgh. His eight-year-old son, Alexander III (1249–1286), eventually succeeded him, and Alan Durward of Coull was appointed his regent. The latter married Marjory, the illegitimate daughter of Alexander II.

Alexander III hunted at Birse and Mar. Celebrations marked Alexander's visit to Deeside with his second wife, Queen Yolande. Days later, his journey south led the king to die in a riding accident. This caused instability, for his heir was an infant, his granddaughter, Margaret 'the Maid of Norway'

(1286–1290). The strategic importance of Deeside and the convictions of Donald, Seventh Earl of Mar, generated the War of Succession and Independence. This tension was sharpened, given that the Maid of Norway (1286–1290) died unexpectedly in Orkney very soon after her accession, thereby leaving no clear heir.

Civil war obtained before this at Alexander III's death, for Robert the Bruce, Earl of Annandale, set a claim against the Maid of Norway. After Margaret's death, 13 other competitors entered the fray, dividing the country and leaving room for Edward I of England to seek the domination of Scotland.

Edward gave Scotland to John Balliol in 1292. King John was unpopular in Scotland and was continually bullied by Edward I. He resigned his crown to the English King, on 10th July, 1296, while the latter was situated at Montrose with his vast army. Days after John's abdication, Edward traversed Crynes Corse Pass into Deeside and by 13th July, 1296, this English army arrived at Durris Castle.

Edward I then stayed at Aberdeen to receive the capitulation of several Deeside barons and then to the Peel of Lumphanan and north through Kintore, Fynnie, Banff, Cullen and Elgin. He returned via Kildrummy by 31st July, then went south to Kincardine o' Neil and camped for one night before fording the Dee and taking the Cairn a' Mounth route into the Mearns, south of Deeside.

Further insurgency caused Edward I's return to Aberdeen on the 23rd August, 1303 via Causey Mounth. He camped at Kincardine o' Neil and later crossed the Cairn a' Mounth to the south, thereby completing his last visit.

Robert the Bruce, (Robert I, 1306–1329), upon losing an encounter in Perth with the English, crossed into Deeside either through Cairnwell Pass to Doldencha or via the Chapel Mounth to Tullich. By July 1306 Bruce was in Aberdeen with his queen, Elizabeth de Burgh, and other members of the royal family.

Hearing that Bruce was in Aberdeen, Edward I mobilised troops under Edward, Prince of Wales, and intended to follow, but expired along the way. Meanwhile, Bruce sent his royal entourage to Kildrummy Castle under charge of his younger brother, Nigel. Bruce travelled to the Deeside hills and then veered south-west.

Edward, Prince of Wales, later Edward II, went through the Fir Mounth on 1st August to lay siege to Kildrummy Castle. Eventually, Osbarn, a blacksmith, created a distraction that allowed the English to gain entry. Nigel got the royal family out and they sought sanctuary in the north, however, the Earl of Ross gave them up to Edward II. Nigel Bruce was later hanged at Berwick. David II (1329–1370), Robert the Bruce's son, was a child of five years upon his accession and this afforded a chance for the English to usurp the Scottish Crown. To this end, Edward III used Edward Balliol just as Edward I had used Balliol's father, John. By August 1332 Balliol landed in Fyfe and in Perthshire to defeat the Scots, and a month later he was crowned King of the Scots. Scotland had two kings, David Bruce and Edward Balliol, a vassal king. The second War of Succession and Independence beckoned.

Balliol alienated his Scottish 'subjects' and after two months fled the country. At this time the English were in Scotland. One force crossed the Causey Mounth route into Deeside. Under the leadership of Sir Thomas Roscelyn, the English ravaged Aberdeen. A pivotal point in the second War of Succession and Independence obtained before the English attack on Aberdeen, the Battle of Culblean, as related in chapter three.

Robert II, Seventh High Steward of Scotland (1370–1390) travelled to Deeside many times, especially to 'Kyndrocht in Marre' – now Braemar. During 1388 he made secret plans in Aberdeen for the invasion of England, which proved successful at Otterburn. Robert II gave the Barony of Kincardine o' Neil and Coull to his third son, Robert, Earl of Fyfe and Menteith.

Robert III's (1390–1406) reign saw vernacular Scots replace Latin in written documents. Although resisted, this move proved advantageous in law and commerce. English sailors captured James I, the only surviving son of Robert III. James was only 11 years of age on March 1406 when Robert III died, and was not released until 1424, long after he had the royal title.

James I (1406–1437) was responsible for subordinating the Earldom of Mar to the crown and thereby limiting the autonomy of the earls. He was subsequently murdered by his uncle, Walter Stewart, Earl of Atholl. James's heart was cut out and taken to the Holy Land and Rhodes before its return by the Knights of St John.

James II (1437–1460) succeeded at six years of age and was 18 by the time he came to Deeside, the year before marrying Marie Gueldres, the only daughter of Arnold, Duke of Gueldres. Queen Marie received a grand reception at Deeside in January 1455. Unhappily, James II also died young at the siege of Roxburgh Castle and this entailed another accession of a minor, James III (1460–1488), James II's his eldest boy, aged nine. James III was concerned with ordinary people more than nobility. He loved the arts, culture and international commerce. Eventually he upset the nobles and was killed on July 1488.

King James III's teenage son was kidnapped before the king's demise, and remained incarcerated for 14 months afterwards. Alexander, the fourth Lord Forbes, accompanied by other barons, appealed to various towns and villages in the north-east of Scotland to raise public interest and seek the rescue of the young king. For emphasis, they used the bloody shirt of James III as a symbol of their cause.

Eventually James IV (1488–1513) was free to visit Deeside while making annual pilgrimages to the shrine of St Dulthus at Tain to pray for the soul of his murdered father. James IV is well remembered through his associations with Old Aberdeen and King's College. James IV's royal charter on 21st August, 1498 established Aberdeen as a royal burgh. He also stayed at the castle of Loch Kinnord in October 1505 and paid his last visit to Deeside in August 1513.

James V (1513–1542) was 18 months old upon his accession and was crowned immediately. Known as 'the poor man's king' he assumed royal authority at fourteen. He wanted to know how 'ordinary' people lived and frequently appeared on Deeside with that aim in mind. At first in 1526 he travelled as a farmer called the 'Gudeman of Ballengeich'. It is said there were several such Deeside visits. Once, near Durris, James and his entourage crossed Cairn a' Mounth Pass. On their way, James asked for shelter from a farmer called Monane Hog. The latter was so entertaining that the king assigned property to Hog and his descendants thereby the Hogs became Lairds of Blairydryne.

Mary Queen of Scots (1542–1567) was greatly associated with Aberdeenshire. This queen was crowned while still an infant and only five years later was sent to France for safety, returning in August 1561. Meanwhile, the Reformation had occurred on 17th August, 1560 and was approved by the Scottish Parliament. Papal jurisdiction was abolished in one week. Mary was devoutly Catholic and henceforth Scotland was open to divisive forces. When the news that Mary, the widow of Francois II of France, was to return, both factions became excited, for each side wanted this queen's support. The Protestants, led by Mary's half-brother, Lord James Stewart, and the Catholics, partly headed by George Gordon, Fourth Earl of Huntly, nurtured mutual hatred. Attempting neutrality for Mary rendered her vulnerable from both sides. Eventually, Lord James Stewart headed off the Protestant Government and Huntly withdrew to Strathbogie, his Aberdeenshire stronghold that is now called Huntly. Huntly met his demise at the Battle of Corrichie, related specifically in chapter three, and it is said Mary overlooked the battle from the Hill o' Fare. However, the latter rumour is unsubstantiated.

Following the battle, other Gordons were guillotined in the Castlegates of Aberdeen, and three days later Sir John Gordon met a similar fate. The corpse of Huntly was embalmed, dressed in sackcloth, shipped to Edinburgh and, six months later, presented before the Privy Council to receive admonition and loss of heraldic entitlement.

Queen Mary abdicated after the battle in favour of her infant son, 13-month-old James VI (1567–1625). James Stewart, Earl of Moray, thus became Regent of Scotland. He was later assassinated in 1569.

James VI assumed government when 11 years of age, and appeared on Deeside granting at least 13 charters. There is another document, a *Commission in Favour of the Provost and Baillies of the Burgh of Aberdeen* of the 2nd February, 1596, which expresses James VI's wish to bring to trial those accused of witchcraft.

James VI nurtured a horror of the latter. In attempting to stop its practice, he wrote *Demonologie, 1597*. The most infamous occurrences of witchcraft were on Deeside. The 1596–1597 records of witch trials in Aberdeen present appalling accounts. James progressed to rages against tobacco and in 1601 published *Counterblast to Tobacco*. Two years later James inherited the throne of England upon Elizabeth I's death, thereby becoming James VI and I. He was followed by his second son, Charles I (1625–1649), who spent the first year of his life at Fyvie Castle.

Charles was devoutly religious and intent upon steering religious policy, hence he confronted both Church and State. In May 1637 he introduced his *Service Book* without seeking validation from either the Scottish Parliament or the General Assembly of the Church of Scotland. In response, the General Assembly enforced subscription to the National Covenant, which upholds Presbyterianism, the democratic governance of the Protestant Church. The subsequent conflict between Royalists and Covenanters appears in the next chapter.

Charles II's (1649–1685) appearance on Deeside in 1650 constituted the last visit to this part of the north-east by a reigning monarch until Victoria in 1848. Charles II remained in exile by virtue of Cromwell until 1660 and was succeeded by his younger brother, James VII and II (1685–1689). The latter was a Catholic king reigning within a Protestant country.

Archibald Campbell, Ninth Earl of Argyll, who had been exiled in Holland, returned to Scotland to lead a rebellion, but was captured and executed. However, the birth of James, Prince of Wales in 1688 signalled another Catholic heir instead of the previously expected accession of the Protestant Princess Mary, wife of Protestant William of Orange.

Any support for James dissipated, and William and Mary were asked to usurp his claim. The offer was accepted and James was exiled. Queen Mary and King William landed in Torbay. Mary II was thus one of only four Scottish queens who were inherent monarchs as distinct from consorts. The others are Mary Queen of Scots, Margaret The Maid of Norway and Queen Anne.

However, matters were later unsettled, for John Graham of Claverhouse, Viscount Dundee, sought clan support for James's cause and the word 'Jacobite' was attributed to supporters of King James VII and II. The north-east became a critical ground of national conflict again and by the end of 1689 a small band of Jacobites marched through the Cairn a' Mounth into Deeside. The subsequent encounters and involvement of the Farquharsons feature in the introductions of other chapters of this book.

William of Orange died on 8th March, 1702 and was succeeded by Queen Anne (1702–1714) the younger daughter of James VII and II. The treaty to unite Scotland and England was signed on 22nd July, 1706 and John Erskine, 24th Earl of Mar, was a signatory. Although he was an erstwhile Jacobite, he was made Secretary of State, which annoyed some of the public, and there was further disquiet upon the accession of George I (1714–1727).

John Erskine offered his services to George, but was rejected. Erskine was known for his 'expedient' loyalties, hence his sobriquet, 'Bobbin' Jock'. Erskine reverted to Jacobite sympathies. The 1715 Jacobite revolt began in Braemar's Castleton. John Erskine and 2000 Highlanders raised a banner for James Francis Edward Stuart, titular King James VIII and III, and son of James VII and II, who died in exile in 1701.

James VIII and III landed at Peterhead in 1716 and joined the Jacobite army in Perth. After the unsuccessful rebellion, James and the Earl of Mar went into exile. John Farquharson was pardoned, but many other Deeside men were executed or enslaved.

By 1745 powerful members of the Farquharson and Gordon estates supported the Hanoverian monarchy, although some supported the Jacobite claims of Charles Edward Stuart. Lord Lewis Gordon had 'kissed the Prince's hand' and was told to raise forces. He attempted to rally support at Aboyne Castle and Blelack House in Cromar, but there was little enthusiasm. However, Francis Farquharson of Monaltrie was appointed Colonel of the Deeside Battalion.

The failure of the 1745 uprising culminated at Culloden Moor. Subsequently, legislation was implemented to suppress the clan system. Highland dress was limited and arms were prohibited; a ruling army of Red Coats enforced these measures.

Charles Stuart died in 1788, his younger brother the titular King Henry IX constituting the last of Royal Stuarts. Henry died on July 1807 and left some of the Crown jewels, taken into exile by James VII and II, to George III (1760–1820), thereby tacitly nominating him worthy Tanist Heir – the heir apparent to the Celtic Chieftains of Scotland.

With Prince Albert's gift of Balmoral Castle to Queen Victoria, and her purchase of Ballochbuie Forest, subsequent members of the royal family, including the present monarchy of Britain, continue this regional connection with kings and queens.

Some lines of royal association have now been sketched around the history of this particular landscape. The next chapter extends that swift drawing to include further instances of violent contest and substantial symbols of defence.

HERITAGE TRAIL

In eighteen hundred and sixty one,
Whilst staying on Deeside,
One Friday morning, the Queen set out,
With her aids and mountain guide.

In her diary she wrote: 'mist in the hills',
'The journey must be doubtful'
But in the valley the sun shone,
The party set off, never fearful.

Incognito and with her aids nearby,
They arrived at Fettercairn.
An archway now stands to mark the spot,
Commemorating her reign.

The next day the party moved on,
Passing the famous Fasque House.
A great example of upstairs and down,
The grounds with deer, pheasant and grouse.

Situated on a wooded plateau,
Not far from the Hill of Fare.
The travellers passed the grounds of Drum,
With the castle high in the air.

On the road from Drum to Tarland,
The castle bade adieu.
The party stopped to admire the scene
Now known as the Queen's View.

Dee and Don – Inspiration

The scent of pine and the sound of water,
The end of the railway line.
The Victorian village of Ballater,
Displays the insignia sign.

Queen Victoria wrote: 'the scene is wild',
'Beautiful and very grand'.
'We saw three hawks and caught seventy trout',
Loch Muick – the finest in the land.

After Albert's death in sixty eight,
In the hope that piece would return,
She built a lodge, called it Glas-Allt Shiel –
The lodge of the grey burn

The end of the trail is near to the Linn,
Where a bridge spans the Dee.
In fifty seven the Queen opened the bridge,
With a toast of Lochnagar Whiskey.

Andrew Whyte

Michael Pegler

King Edward VII Statue, Aberdeen

David Gowans

John Brown, Queen Victoria's Aide

The Hunting Party

Alan King

Dee and Don – Inspiration

The Queen's View

DAVID ROBERTSON

Queen Victoria and John Brown at Balmoral Castle
Mary Evans Picture Library

Balmoral Castle

BL Images Limited

Michael Pegler

Chapter 3

Battles and Castles

The land framed by the rivers Dee and Don has provided a dramatic stage upon which various private and public interests have been contested. Partisan allegiances to inherited authority, or attachments concurrent with religious faith, have generated violent events and, as a consequence, the region has many instances of defensive architecture. Therefore, this introduction will summarise such instances of battles and descriptions of castles that are extant in the landscape of the Dee and Don.

This region has witnessed battles throughout its history including conflicts with Roman legions. For example, there is some evidence to suppose that the lowland hill of Bennachie is near the site of *Mons Graupius*, the clash between Gnaeus Julius Agricola's forces and early Caledonian tribes (AD 84–85). The campaigns of Emperor Septimius Severus may also have occurred here (AD 208–212). However, it is impossible to remark upon every instance of conflict, and this account has limited summaries to three well-documented examples for each river valley.

An altercation between John Gordon, the Earl of Huntly's third son, and James Ogilvie of Cardell resulted in a duel. Ogilvie was badly injured. Gordon escaped arrest and fled to Aberdeenshire. This event indirectly led to the Battle of Corrichie between the forces of Mary Queen of Scots and George Gordon, Earl of Huntly.

Queen Mary was visiting northern Scotland in August 1562 with Lord James Stewart, Huntly's enemy. Upon reaching Aberdeen the Countess of Huntly tried to mediate for her son, Sir John Gordon, by inviting Mary to Huntly's seat at Strathbogie Castle. These overtures were rejected and Mary insisted upon Sir John Gordon's submission. Sir John Gordon initially surrendered, but the subsequent knowledge of imminent imprisonment at Sterling Castle by Lord Erskine, the uncle of Sir James Stewart, prompted another escape.

Mary then granted Lord James Stewart the Earldom of Moray, entitlements informally held by Huntly. Mary also outlawed Huntly and his sons, severely compromising Huntly's goodwill towards her.

By now Huntly's anger and insecurity motivated him to amass support and he marched upon Aberdeen from Strathbogie. Huntly's army progressed through Garioch and headed towards Echt, passing Kintore. They camped near Cullerlie to the south of Loch Skene, subsequently called Gordon's Moss.

James Stewart, also predicting trouble, marched from Aberdeen on 27th October, 1562 with George Hay, Seventh Earl of Erroll, William, Seventh Lord Forbes and John, Prior of Coldingham. Their well-armed force of 2,000 men included cavalry and Lothian spearsmen. Upon reaching Garlogie, ten miles west of Aberdeen, they camped for the night.

By the following dawn the opposing forces were very near one another. Led by Forbes, Moray's front line attacked the fringes of Huntly's force. The Gordons then retreated to higher ground, east of the Hill o' Fare. To reach that place, Huntly headed up Landerberry Burn, to what is now called Gordon's Howe, while continually being harried by Forbes' band of skirmishers. Meanwhile, the bulk of Moray's army went west, tracing the current B9125 and B977, thereby arresting Huntly's retreat and the advantage of higher ground. Moray achieved this by following Corrichie Burn and attaining the Hill o' Fare to the west of Huntly's situation at Gordon's Howe. The area was covered in forest then, so both forces were strategically equal.

The Gordon Highlanders charged, and Moray's infantry confronted this assault. However, the latter then pretended to retreat and the subsequent assumption of victory persuaded Huntly to regroup. Unknown to Huntly, there were traitors in his ranks and, upon a prepared signal, the Gordons of Haddo put a sprig of heather in their bonnets to differentiate themselves. Upon Huntly's second charge, the Haddo Gordons turned upon Huntly's forces, but still defiant in the face of this treachery, Huntly resumed his charge, although this time they fell upon Lothian spears. Once Moray's cavalry had hunted down the broken force of Huntly the Battle of Corrichie had ended.

The opposing forces of Sir Andrew de Moray and David of Strathbogie, Earl of Atholl, fought at the Battle of Cublean near Dinnet on 30th November, 1335, St Andrew's Day. Indeed it was Andrew's day in a different sense, for Moray won this significant encounter of the second War of Succession and Independence.

Sir Andrew was charged with the guardianship of Robert the Bruce's son, David II. However, the Earl of Atholl had aspirations to take the throne, and his treachery prompted this particular conflict. While David II was abroad, Atholl laid siege to the rest of the royal family at Kildrummy Castle, the seat of the Earldom of Mar at that time. When Moray heard this he gathered forces in the Lothians to meet the challenge and was accompanied by Patrick, Second Earl of March, Sir William of Douglas, 'Knight of Liddesdale', and other important personages. They speedily marched north via the Fir Mounth Pass into Deeside by the Mill of Dinnet.

Atholl, aware of the threat, marched south from Kildrummy to camp his 3,000-strong army at the Vat Burn on the east face of Cublean Hill. It is suggested that Moray had similar forces of 800 mounted Knights of Lothian and probably 3,000 other armed forces. By 29th November, Atholl was camped on the road, now the A97, between Logie Coldstone and the woodland called the Cambus o' May. It is said that Moray saw the glimmering of Atholl's campfire as he passed their situation, and also set up camp.

The respective armies were well matched and neither had superior positions, the camps facing one another over two miles, west to east. An offensive course was apparent, for there was a clear trail that ran between lochs Kinnord and Davan, thereby traversing extant marshes and forestation.

Meeting with Moray on the evening of 29th November, John of Craig contributed his topographical knowledge to the battle plan. Sir William of Douglas was to lead the frontal attack from the east between the two lochs while a second would ensue from the north-west, led by Moray. The latter position was to be guided by John of Craig travelling across country north of Loch Davan. This would bring them to Cublean Hill above Atholl's ranks and from where the second charge would be instigated. Sir William crossed

Ordie Moss as planned and paused east and south of Logie Coldstone. The undulations of the land secreted both strategic situations.

In the morning Sir William's men overtook Atholl's sentries before the alarm was raised. Upon confronting Sir William, Atholl thought he detected sufficient hesitation to withdraw and gain advantage at Vat Burn, towards the ford. This proved to be a disastrous blunder because Moray and John of the Craig then closed upon their ranks from above. Ferocious fighting ensued, but soon Atholl's men were scattered in the face of the two-pronged attack. Robert de Brady and Sir William Conwyn were killed at the ford. Alexander Gordon killed Atholl and became the next Laird of Strathbogie.

By September 1651, Cromwell's Roundheads were established at Castlehill in Aberdeen. After a section of General Monk's forces entered the region via the Causey Mounth, on 10th February, 1654, Royalists led by Lord Glengairn and Kenmure, with Sir Ewan Cameron of Lochiel, approached Tullich. This instigated a Roundhead force, commanded by Colonel Thomas Morgan. The latter encountered 1,500 Royalist troops moving to marshy ground where the Roundheads did not want to pursue them, meanwhile Lochiel's Highlanders controlled the Ballater Pass. Morgan engaged the Royalists there, but Lochiel's bowmen slaughtered many of Morgan's men, although some reached the higher face of Craigendorroch. This tactic forced Lochiel to retreat westwards to exposed ground at which point the Roundheads overpowered their enemy. This conflict constituted the last time a long bow featured in battle.

The Battle of Harlaw entailed the opposing forces of Alexander Stewart, Earl of Mar and Donald, Lord of the Isles. It took place on 24th July, 1411 near Inverurie. This is one of the best-known, longest and bloodiest battles in Scottish history. Not everything about the battle is clear, but the following gives us some notion at least.

Donald, Lord of the Isles led Highlanders into the lowlands towards Aberdeen. Alexander Stewart, Earl of Mar and son of the 'Wolf of Badenoch', convened the barons of Aberdeen, Angus and the Mearns led a lowland army near Inverurie. Donald, having overtaken Garioch, reached three miles west of Inverurie to be halted by the lowland force. The fighting lasted until darkness precluded further action. The highlanders withdrew from a battle site drenched in blood. The lowlanders were too tired to pursue them.

It is said more than 1,000 highlanders lost their lives, but the cost was equally heavy on both sides.

On 2nd July, 1645 there was another significant battle this time at Alford between a Royalist army led by the Marquis of Montrose and a Covenanter force led by Major-General William Baillie. The battle site incorporates Latch Howe, north-west of Alford, Feight Faulds, east of Tough and Bloody Faulds, west of Boglouster Wood.

The armies were of equitable force, although it is said Baillie had more cavalry than Montrose. This superiority was offset by the attendance of the 'Committee of Estates', who were authorised to interrupt Baillie's command. This administering body of the National Covenant included various earls and Calvinist clergymen.

Montrose secreted in a position above the Don's Montgarrie ford, at Alford. Baillie, was averse to crossing the ford, perceiving vulnerability before he could attain a battle formation. However, Baillie's cavalry commander, Lord Balcarres, pressed the committee's influence to engage with the enemy as soon as possible even though it entailed a boggy passage through the ford.

Montrose waited until the Covenanter's Cavalry was across the river and its infantry was still crossing before unleashing his attack. A bloody conflict ensued between the Covenant Cavalry and the Royalist Cavalry, under Lord Gordon. Montrose then used a reserve force of Gordon infantry, and the Covenanter ranks broke. Any escape across the ford was an arduous course to take, and utter carnage resulted. The Royalists won the day, but they had lost Lord Gordon, and a stone was set to mark his demise in the battlefield.

The Battle of Barra Hill on Christmas Eve, 1307 was a significant campaign that marked a pivotal point in the War of Succession and Independence. The site is at Oldmeldrum, near Inverurie.

In February 1306 Robert the Bruce and his allies murdered John Comyn, Lord of Badenoch. Comyn was a nephew of the former King John Balliol. This death motivated those loyal to Comyn to consider Bruce an enemy and resist his accession. Those previously focused upon the struggle against the English invasion now considered Robert the greater threat. The main protagonist in this regard was Comyn's cousin, John Comyn, Third Earl of Buchan.

Coalitions against Robert the Bruce were so strong that he probably would have been defeated but for the death of Edward I of England in July 1307. Edward II became concerned with home affairs, and abandoned his Scottish allies just when they needed the English army. Spotting this window of opportunity, Robert moved quickly.

Robert the Bruce's brother had hanged at Berwick. King Robert had to spend the winter of 1306 eluding the English army. However, by the spring of 1307 he faced his enemies and by the autumn he was on Deeside prowling Aberdeen and Comyns, the Earl of Buchan.

Bruce's health was failing, for apart from fatigue he had leprosy. It is said that his brother, Edward Bruce, took temporary charge. His army was camped at Inverurie near Oldmeldrum. On 22nd December Buchan was ready to attack Bruce, but these first efforts proved ineffectual. However, on the dawn of the 23rd, David de Brechin launched another attack, but the decisive moment eluded them, for Brechin's men were the only force ready.

Although still ill, Bruce arose to prepare a counter-attack. As his enemy approached, Buchan set his army across the road to Inverurie between Barra Hill and Lochter Burn marshes; some unreliable conscripts were at the rear while his knights and men-at-arms were placed at the front. The conscripts were told that Bruce was too ill to engage the battle in person and when Bruce took to the field Buchan's men were unnerved at the sight. Buchan tried to stabilise the line of his troops, but soon he also fled, chased by Bruce's men to Fyvie. In fact the earl escaped to England, where he met his death the same year. The Battle of Inverurie ended opposition to King Robert in Aberdeenshire. However, he did not intend to leave any potential hostility towards his authority and took bloody action to ensure that strategic position.

Both the Dee and Don valleys are strewn with castles and fortified houses. Early fortifications are constituted in examples of hill forts and crannogs, strongholds on lochs or boggy land, within which whole communities established their security. The first private castles were made of timber upon earthwork mounds, categorised as motte and bailey castles. Examples of such mounds are the Peel of Lumphanan and the Bass near Inverurie. In general, castle styles may be described in terms of their plan view. These include 'enclosure plan', 'keep tower', 'L plan', 'link plan' and 'Z plan'.

Corgarff Castle in upper Donside is said to have been a hunting seat of the Earl of Mar. Initially, the structure was just an enclosed tower house built by John Forbes of Towie in 1550. It proved to be strategically important throughout history.

In 1607 bandits used Corgarff then it became an estate of John Erskine, 18th Earl of Mar in 1626. In 1645, the castle was utilised by James Graham, First Marquis of Montrose and commander of the Royalist forces during the Civil War. During 1689 Corgarff was burned down by Jacobites to prevent it being used by William of Orange supporters.

In 1715 John Erskine instigated the Jacobite rising from Kildrummy Castle, and subsequently came to Corgarff to organise his army before marching on Braemar. After the defeat of the 1715, rising government forces burned down Corgarff, and the Earl of Mar's estates were taken.

The 1745 uprising produced the Corgarff Castle we see today. The effort to suppress the Highlanders entailed government outposts throughout the country. In 1748 Corgarff Castle became a barracks. Its structure acquired pavilions and an unusual star-shaped enclosing wall as in the design of Braemar Castle. In 1802 Corgarff was used as a farmhouse and was reacquired by the government in 1827 to control the smuggling and local distillation of whisky. The army finally left in 1831. The last occupiers were the Ross sisters, known locally as the 'castle ladies', who left during the 1914–1918 World War.

Standing ten miles from Alford, Kildrummy was one of the largest castles in Scotland. Gilbert De Moravia, Bishop of Caithness, may have constructed the castle at the bidding of Alexander II in the 13th century. However, its oldest part dates from the 12th century.

Kildrummy Castle's central tower of 1172 would have impressed. For good reason it was called 'The Snow Tower', standing five storeys high and constructed from white freestone. The castle later developed the aspect of a shield with six separate towers. Earthworks afforded protection and it incorporated a dry moat with a very deep ravine. Excavations in 1925 revealed ornate stone flooring and signs of previous battles. The castle's foundations and lower walls may still be seen.

Kildrummy was the main fortification of the ancient Garioch province and an ancient royal lineage. It was a domain of David Earl of Huntingdon,

William I's brother. It then came to Robert I (Robert the Bruce), then through his sister's marriage to the Earldom of Mar.

After the 1715 Jacobite Rebellion, John, Earl of Mar lost his land to the Crown. The castle then belonged to the Erskine family for a time, but John Gordon of Wardhouse eventually bought Kildrummy Castle in 1731. It was besieged several times in history and many notable people have spent time there including Edward I, William Wallace, Robert the Bruce's queen and daughter Margery, Nigel Bruce and David II. Historic Scotland now owns the remains of the castle.

From one of the largest castles to one of the smallest, Terpersie was once called Dalpersie. It is found in Tullynessie parish in a valley of the Coreen hills. Designed according to the 'Z plan' style of castle it is now a ruin and would have been surrounded by a moat. Terpersie was built by William Gordon, the eighth son of James Gordon of Lesmore, and participant in the Battle of Corrichie in 1563 and Tillyangus in 1574, where he slew the brother of Lord Forbes, 'Black Arthur'. The Gordons of Terpersie fought in the 1745 insurgence, for which the last laird was executed.

Lickleyhead Castle is near Insch village, built in 1629 by Forbes of Leslie, subsequent to obtaining the land from Henry Leith of Barns. The Forbeses of Lickleyhead were impassioned Covenanters. In 1701 the castle passed to the Hays and in 1723 to the Duffs of Craigston. The castle was then acquired, in turn, by the Gordons, the Ogilvies and Lumsdens of Auchindoir. Styled according to the 'L plan', the castle incorporates an extended wing that affords protection to two sides of the main building. This castle is in good condition, retaining oval windows in the angle-turrets, which also feature in Castle Fraser.

The extant Braemar Castle replaced Kindrochit, which was the hunting seat of Robert II in the late 14th century. Built by John Erskine, the Seventh Earl of Mar, to resist the Farquharsons, the Tower House dates from 1628. Braemar burned down in 1689 and John Erskine was killed by the 'Black Colonel', John Farquharson of Inverey. The Farquharsons acquired Braemar Castle in 1732 and ownership remains in that family.

The architect, John Adam, converted it to a Hanoverian fort to be leased to the War Office after the second Jacobite Rebellion. In 1797 the castle reverted again to the Farquharson clan. The current Braemar Castle is of the

'L plan' style with angle-turrets. A star-shaped curtain wall surrounds it, and the principal entrance has an original iron lattice gate or *yett*.

The National Trust for Scotland now holds Crathes Castle near Banchory, bequeathed by Sir James Burnett of Leys in 1951. The castle is situated upon land granted by King Robert the Bruce in 1323. During the 14th and 15th centuries the Burnetts of Leys first constructed a timber fort upon an island amid a bog – a *crannog*. Alexander Burnett finished the current tower house of Crathes Castle in 1596 and another wing was attached in the 18th century. This harled castle was also built in an 'L plan' style by the Burnetts of Leys. Interruptions in its building have presented some unusual features including an oversized stair tower. Both round and square turrets crown the building. Elaborate corbels and various gargoyles animate the external structure.

Drum Castle is probably the oldest occupied castle in Scotland. The 24th and final Laird of Drum, Henry Quentin Forbes Irvine, left it to the National Trust for Scotland. It has belonged to the Irvine family for over 650 years. The building comprises an original stone tower built during the reign of Alexander III of the mid-13th century. Alexander, the Ninth Laird of Drum, had built the connected stone mansion and Jacobean house in 1619. Its Third Laird, Sir Alexander of Drum, died at the Battle of Harlaw.

The castle constituted a watchtower in the Royal Forest of Drum. Exceeding 60 feet in height the four-sided tower has rounded corners to glance away attacks. The mason was probably Richard Cementarius, 'Richard the Mason'. There are three stone vaults above one another. The walls of the basement are 10 feet thick. A well is situated in one corner of the basement, the latter having been a dungeon or storeroom. The staircase, within the wall, rises to the great hall and would have been entered by an exterior door approached by ladder.

Adjoining a Jacobean house, the tower is divided to provide an upper chamber or solar, separated by a wooden floor. Beneath the upper vault occurs the large hall, also consisting of two chambers, wherein extant corbels remain to support the floor. This magnificent hall has a pointed vault elevated 21 feet. The vault's structure mirrors the arch of a famous bridge in Aberdeen, Brig o' Balgownie. It is thought Richard Cementarius recycled wooden templates in both tasks.

The content of this account has been associated with broader notions of establishing, expanding or defending partisan interests and influences. Sometimes such ideals entail the overcoming of natural boundaries to gain tactical advantage. Rivers may present such natural obstacles as significant as a mountainous landscape. The various means by which humans have thwarted the barriers presented by the rivers Dee and Don are to be considered in the next chapter.

THE HUNTED

We cleared our muskets as we sat around in the clearing, and while we waited, we talked of the man we sought.

"He's a MacGregor and son of a chieftain", said one Redcoat.

"It's said he's descended from King Kenneth", said another.

Other men added what they knew, until we had the whole story – or most of it.

The MacGregors had long since been evicted by the Campbells – those same infamous Campbells of the Glencoe killings. Now landless, the MacGregors were known as the 'Children of the Mist'. Following this latest rebellion of 1715, Jacobites were being rounded up. Today, it was the Jacobite Robert MacGregor that we hunted, 'though some said that his only allegiance was to liberty. There were tales of how he went to the aid of those who were in trouble with the law, or with their landlords. The man was no saint, however, and had rustled cattle with the best of them.

There came a shout. A look-out had spotted our prey, and the clearing emptied as we took up the chase. Crashing through trees and over rough ground, we caught sight now and then of his red hair or the tartan of his kilt.

There was no escape for him. Ahead, the River Dee ran through a deep gorge. As we neared it, I could hear the roar and thunder of the water as it plunged between the high rock-faces on either side. We came to a halt above him and watched as he bounded down the rocks to certain death.

Then like a deer he leapt, like an eagle he soared and, landing safe on the far side, disappeared into the woods.

A bridge now crosses the river at Peterculter, where Rob Roy MacGregor made his famous leap. On the rocks above the gorge stands the statue of a red-haired Highlander.

MARTHA BOTTRELL

MEN O' LONACH

A-doon the glen, the Lonach Men
Mairch on, as if tae war.
The Wallace clan, the Forbes men;
Challenge, gin ye daur!

Heids held heich an faces strang,
Clan tartans bricht an swingin.
The beat o' drum an bagpipe sang
Set sleepin hills a – ringin.

Ilka bonnet wears a gaithered sprig
O' heather fite or slip o' green.
This day, Tradition mairches o'er the Brig,
The morn, thon Strath will near be teem.

Wi whisky drams tae warm their kites,
The chiels mairch doon the valley.
A forest grey o' bristlin pikes,
True Scotsmen, rise an rally!

Mairch on for aye, ye Lonach Men
Aside yer ripplin river.
Ye stir the bleed o' Hielenmen,
"Ho! Ho! Lonach!" Battlecry for iver.
For Scotia, Wallace an de Brus!

MARY MUNRO

ODE TO CRAIGIEVAR CASTLE
By a National Trust Guide

O Craigievar, I bless the day I spoke tae Dave and asked
If I could tak the tourists roon, an spik aboot your past.
When they come in the studded door, far dungeon's on their richt,
The guard room's fair afore them, wi the kitchen oot o sicht.

The granite steps lead tae the Hall, I gie them aa the spiel
O Danzig Willie an his wife, I learnt it at the squeel.
Across the wye's Withdrawin Room, far leddies o lang syne
Wid sit an hae a news afore they'd tak a gless o wine.

The Tartan Room is up the stairs, wi portraits aa aroon,
O Danzig Willie, Reed Sir John an Bishop Patrick's loon.
Syne up again an throu the place far housekeepers wid bide,
Intae the Queen's Room far the bed fair taks the place o pride.

Anither race o stairs an syne the castle widens oot
Tae corbellin an towers aroon, an mony a fancy spoot.
The Blue Room his an eerie feel o spirits nae at ease.
Did Reed Sir John regret the deed that made the Gordon cease?

The Nursery is a fair-sized room, wi sleepin quarters next,
Far little Forbeses did their sums, an likewise learnt their text.
Abeen them aa the Lang Room lies, it faces North an Sooth,
Wi tales o washin hingin there, passed on by word o mooth.

Next door the servant quines wid sleep: box beds held three or four
An by the Secret Stair we'd gang doon tae the first floor.
Back in the Great Hall tae admire the stucco ceiling there
An up abeen the muckle fire the coat o airms sae rare.

Syne doon we gang tae dungeons dark, far peer souls wid hae pined
While leddies up abeen their heids, had been baith wined an dined.
Then, oot the studded door an yett, tae hae an outside view,
Remindin aa o fairy tales. Craigievar! A toast tae you.

LORNA ALEXANDER

Michael Pegler

Crathes Castle

Corgarff Castle

David Robertson

Michael Pegler

Chapter 4

Crossing rivers

The places where rivers are crossed correspond to junctures between many points of departure and destination. The Grampian uplands or 'The Mounth' admit several routes across Deeside and into Donside. The historian, Fenton Wyness, mentions there were eight important examples.

The Causey Mounth linked the south with Formartine in the north and crossed the Dee at Aberdeen. Elsick Mounth, a spur of the Causey Mounth, which led to the Garioch region and crossed the Dee just west of Peterculter. Cryne's Corse joined Laurenceburg with the Garioch, crossing the Dee just east of Durris. The Cairn a' Mounth divided before reaching Strachan and connected Fettercairn to Donside and the north, the latter crossing at Kincardine o' Neil along its western fork and Banchory along its eastern fork. The Fir Mounth divided in three before reaching Deeside, and crossed to the west of Ballater, Tullich and the Mill of Dinnet. Capel Mounth linked Forfar in the south with Donside, passing through the west of Ballater. Finally, the Tolmounth joined with the Cairnwell and linked Perth with Strathspey via Braemar. The extension of these trails across the Dee was contingent upon the emergence of fords and ferries. The latter became established a long time before there were bridges, and even by 1800 only four bridges obtained over the Dee.

Apart from some private boats, at the time of his publication, Fenton Wyness also lists 27 public river ferries on the Dee. Three of these were in Aberdeen: a lower ferry at the harbour, functioning before 1648; an upper ferry that gave its name to the district of Ferryhill and a ferry below the Bridge of Dee, which was disused after 1527. A ferry operated between Blairs College and Bieldside on the north bank of the Dee. The charge was one penny. Sometimes called the Heathcot Ferry, it was managed by a family called Main. When her father died, Bella Main acquired the sobriquet, 'Ferry Bell', upon taking over management of the ferry, which closed in the early 1960s.

Wyness provides an extensive list of ferries and fords that were once active across the Dee. Some of the fords and ferries were still in use by the late sixties, such as: Long-Ford at the Mill of Coull, Braemar; Ardearg Ford, west of Braemar; Invercauld Ford and Inverchandlick Ford, west of Braemar Castle; Girnock Ford at Strathgirnock; Kincardine o' Neil Ferry and Ford; Blairs Ferry at Bieldside and Castletown Ferry west of Braemar Castle.

There are several bridges over the Dee in Aberdeen. The Wellington Suspension Bridge, also called the Chain Bridge, was opened in 1830 and was designed by Samuel Brown. It superseded Craiglug Ferry and was the sole connection to Torry until 50 years later when the opening of the Victoria Bridge afforded a better link following the death of 32 people in a terrible ferry boat accident. The Victoria Bridge, by Edward Blyth, also transferred gas and water over the river to the suburb of Torry. Wellington Bridge was closed to vehicles after the Queen Elizabeth II Bridge was opened in 1984; however, the former endured as a footbridge for awhile longer.

The Old Bridge of Dee, the brainchild of Bishop Elphinstone, provided the main southerly entrance to Aberdeen. Bishop Gavin Dunbar realised the plans, and construction took place between 1520 and 1527. Although it has been altered over the centuries, the 16th century piers and various coats of arms that adorn the bridge are preserved. The semicircles that constitute the structural integrity of its seven ridged arches remain very impressive. The structure is aligned to road level, and passing places are inset above the piers for the safety of pedestrians. A chapel was built on the north end and in 1545 a gateway was added to the southern end as a toll gate. In 1842 the width was increased to almost 26 feet. Subsequently, in 1941, the King George VI Bridge was erected farther downstream to serve Aberdeen.

Designed by John Smith, St Devenick's Bridge or 'Shakkin' Briggie' was constructed in 1837 from the finances of Dr George Morison of Elsick, who was the minister of Banchory-Devenick Church between 1785 and 1845. The bridge superseded the boat that previously served as transport to unite the congregation. The bridge was intended to secure full attendance at church services. The floods of 1958 undermined the foundations, so the bridge was closed.

Divided by the River Dee, the late 13th century parishes of Peterculter and Maryculter were connected by a ferry and the Coblestock Ford. The erection of Maryculter Bridge in 1895 afforded service to the Milltimber Station from the south and was originally called the Mill Inn Bridge. During the extremes of the 1937 flood, on the 25th January, it is said that the road across the bridge was beneath 4 feet of water.

Park Bridge was originally a toll bridge on the road between the Deeside Turnpike and the Parish of Durris. The Deeside Railway Company provided this connection to attract business from south of the river in 1854. They charged a halfpenny for pedestrians, a penny for cyclists and threepence for automobiles. This was the last toll bridge in Aberdeenshire, and continued until the middle of the 1950s. The toll house is still to be found on the north bank.

Looking to the southern end of Park Bridge, an octagonal tower can be seen, mistakenly called Keith's Tower. The Duke of Gordon built it in 1825 to mark his gaining the Durris estate. Keith's Muir, an area on the north bank of the river, was the site of a conflict in the 14th century between the Irvines of Drum and the Keiths, Great Marischals of Scotland. The latter were the proprietors of estates south of the river. Although the Irvines prevailed, the subsequent marriage between their families signalled the end of their feud. In 2002, a ceremony of goodwill between the Irvines and Keiths was enacted upon Park Bridge between Michael Keith, Earl of Kintore, the Chief of the Clan Keith, and David Irvine, 26th Laird of Drum.

It is thought that Thomas the Doorward, father of Alan Durward, constructed the first bridge over the Dee at Kincardine o' Neil in 1220. This date is an approximation and could easily be revised to the year 1230. The records also leave some room for uncertainty regarding whether the bridge was of timber or stone construction, although probability favours the former assumption. The subsequent bridge at Kincardine o' Neil, The Potarch Bridge, was built around 1814, three years after the Bridge of Alford. Designed by Thomas Telford, these bridges were connected by a stretch of new road in 1817. The contractor, William Minto of Alford, carried out all three projects. Potarch Bridge comprises a granite construction of three arches that cross 200 feet of waterway and include a middle span of 68 feet. The route, which shadows the Cairn a' Mounth trail, has been referred to as 'The Huntly Road' or the 'North and South Road'.

A ferry and a ford at Aboyne were essential, given its proximity to key routes through Deeside. The ford was a few hundred feet from the bridge, and farther upstream, slightly east of the bridge, occurred a notable ferry called the 'Ferry of Bontie' (or Bowntie). Until 1827 the ferry had been in use, but on the evening of 'Michael's fair', in October, a sudden deluge brought about the death of a woman and her daughter travelling on the crowded ferry. In 1828 the Earl of Aboyne built a suspension bridge, but this was never completed because of the flood of 1829. However, in 1831 on the same site a bridge was built bearing the Gordon coat of arms. The current bridge is the third to be completed on this site and was finished in 1871.

In the second half of the 18th century Ballater was a new village in need of a bridge. This need was eventually satisfied near the site of the old ford and ferry on the Fir Mounth. The old route, 'the Crags of Ballater', extended from Tullich through the pass of Ballater, crossing the River Gairn by an ancient packhorse bridge. George Chalmers notes a Roman road from the Crags of Ballater to Corgarff in 1807 as 'The Commutation Road'.

In 1828 William Farquaharson made a small bridge over the Loin Burn to provide access to quarry for stone, silver and lead. The first bridge of Ballater was built in 1783, but was destroyed by the flood of 1799. It was said to have been a beautiful granite structure to the east of the present bridge. The second bridge was by Thomas Telford with three arches, the middle span exceeding 60 feet. The bridge, started in 1807 and finished in 1809, was destroyed in another deluge in 1829. In 1833 a timber bridge was planned and approved by Telford. It was completed by 1834 and was built from Braemar timber just west of the previous site, serving for a further 50 years. The new bridge of granite was built to the west and opened in 1889 by Queen Victoria. It was designed by the architectural engineers, Jenkins and Marr, and built by John Fyfe of Kemnay.

In 1804 the Reverend Alexander Henderson relocated the Church of Crathie from its site near the ferry of Clachanturn to the side of the old Deeside road. Thirty years later the ferry ceased operating and the extant footbridge was constructed, a cast iron suspension bridge. About 2600 feet west of the latter, Prince Albert provided Balmoral Bridge by 1858, at the east entrance of the Balmoral estate.

There is also an old bridge over the Crathie Burn, part of the old Deeside road, which extended through Glen Gairn to Corgarff, Tommintoul and Grantown-on-Spey and on to Fort George. This military road incorporating part of the B976 and on through the A939 was associated with the General Wade's military road. The old Invercauld Bridge also described as General Wade's Bridge extends west to Braemar and the Cairnwell Mounth and was built in 1752. Wade was commander-in-chief of George I's force in Scotland for 11 years until 1737. He built 250 roads and 40 bridges in the Highlands, but none in Deeside or Donside. Wade was sent to Flanders before the 'new' military roads of 1744 and 1770 and he was dead before the military roads were finished.

The bridge at Invercauld dates from 1752 and the bridge of Clunie near Braemar, which links Auchendryne and Castletown, is dated from 1863. Made of granite, the latter is of a truly beautiful and concise design. It is attributed to the architect, Reid, from Elgin, William Knight, an Aberdonian architect, and contractor John Fife of Kemnay. The bridge sits on the site of the ancient timber bridge of Robert II's reign, in the 14th century, which gave the place its ancient name, *Kindrochaid* – 'End of the Bridge' and the origins of Braemar.

There is a ford situated near the start of the Don at an elevation of 1930 feet and to the west of Delnadamph Lodge. As the road peters out to a rough trail another track heads towards the valley of the River Avon. Pursuing this direction entails crossing the Don at the Ford of Culhachathadh. The first bridges encountered while travelling east from the Don's source is at the Bridge-end of Allargue. The attendant inn used to be in a hamlet near a hill called The Cock. The owners advertised their inn with a Red Cock sign. The latter eventually betokened a bridge as the result of soldiers from nearby Corgarff Castle asking for the inn by the bridge, or Cock Bridge. Allargue Bridge is of beam and slab construction spanning 30 feet, and at Cock Bridge is a single arch of stonework.

There are other bridges near the A939. At an elevation of 1400 feet occurs Luib Bridge, which displays a double masonry arch with filled spandrels and a maximum span of over 40 feet. There is a tale associated with this crossing place to be related in chapter eight, along with other stories and legends.

At Colnabachin there is a bridge of beam and slab construction spanning 41 feet, and travelling farther east, along the A944, we come to the western end of the Castle Newe estate where there is a cast iron arch. This bridge has three spans with a maximum span of 68 feet. The Bridge of Newe and the Bridge of Buckham at the eastern end of the grounds of Castle Newe, were erected between 1856 and 1858. The Bridge of Buckham entails two masonry arches with filled spandrels and a maximum span of 50 feet. An eirde house, or earth house, containing various archaeological artefacts was found near here. There is more about the construction of eirde houses in the next chapter.

John Inverernan built the Bridge of Poldulie, or Pooldhulie. It is a single masonry arch with filled spandrels built in 1715, and occurs over the upper Don, west of Bellabeg. It connects the main road to the north of the river with the old turnpike on the south side. Many observers comment upon the elegance of its single arch, which spans 40 feet. The structural integrity of this beautiful stone bridge was confirmed by its survival of the great flood of 1829.

There are several constructions of reinforced concrete beam and slab. The bridge at Milltown of Towie consists of four spans with a maximum span of 50 feet. Glenkindie Bridge has lattice side panels and two spans with a maximum span of 41 feet. Culfork Bridge, built in 1990, occurs on an unclassified road and is a double span construction with the maximum single span of 34 feet. The Don Bridge at Bellabeg has a single 60 feet span made from steel truss panels and was also erected in 1990.

Seeking a contrast to these newer bridges, we follow the River Don as it meanders near the 'The Corbies' or Coillebhar Hill. This is said to be near the site of St. Machar's Chapel to the south of where the Don forms Machar's Haugh. Chapel Haugh and Chapel Ford present us with ancient places of worship.

As we progress towards the middle reaches of the Don we come to the Bridge of Alford, situated on the A944. As its name suggests, this was once the site of a ford. It was also a ferry known as the 'Boat of Forbes', named after the proprietors of the estate. The bridge comprises three stone arches, with filled spandrels, crossing 144 feet with a maximum single span of 49 feet. As mentioned earlier, this bridge was designed by Thomas Telford and built by William Minto in 1811. It is significant, apart from its impressive physical aspect, for it completes the 'North and South Road' with Potarch Bridge on Deeside.

Montgarrie Bridge, in close proximity to Alford, has a double span of lattice trusses and steel channelling. It has a maximum span of 49 feet. East of Montgarrie, we may come across the Grecian style of Whitehaugh House. Just a short distance east is the disused 'Highlanders Ford' and 'Highlanders Haugh'. The latter is associated with the famous Battle of Harlaw and the crossing of Montrose's army, prior to the Battle of Alford, mentioned in chapter three.

Progressing east, on the B992 near Castle Forbes is the Bridge of Keig. This is an elegant construction that dates from 1817. It consists of a single stone arch, with filled spandrels over 98 feet, and downstream there is a suspended footbridge of steel cable and timber decking.

The frequency of crossing places continues, and further examples include The Don Bridge at Monymusk, which incorporates a steel beam and concrete slab construction. It consists of two spans with a maximum span of 60 feet. Using the same construction materials as the latter, Culquoich Bridge has three spans with a maximum span of 32 feet. The Don is subsequently crossed at Burnhervie in a single span by a suspended footbridge constructed with steel cables and a timber deck. At Inverurie the A96, on the Inverurie bypass, crosses the Don, although there is an older bridge on the B993. There is also a rail bridge at Port Elphinstone, Inverurie.

There is an attractive single arch to be found in Kemnay Bridge that clears over 120 feet, built in 1930. Nearby, the bridge at Kintore presents a single steel and concrete bow arch of 150 feet, built in 1985. This bridge, at the Boat of Kintore, supplants the old bridge at Kintore, which had cast figures on its girders betokening the arms of the Earl of Kintore and these were reproduced on the girders of the new bridge. The Boat of Kintore refers to the old ferry operating across the Don. The ferryman, George Marnoch, or 'Boatie Marnoch', was a well-known citizen of Kintore.

The Boat of Hatton lies along the current B979 and as the name suggests was also the site of a ferry. This bridge is of a reinforced concrete beam and slab construction suspended over three spans, with a maximum span of 124 feet. Made in 1934 it exhibits the style of art deco, associated with the period. It is one of two sister bridges with the same design in Aberdeenshire. The other is over the River Dee at Dinnet, which was designed in 1933 by W A Fairhursts and completed in 1935. They incorporate an unusual configuration of cantilevers.

The Brig o' Balgownie was originally called the Bridge of Don and is situated in the older district of Aberdeen. It was either Bishop Henry Cheyne or Robert the Bruce who ordered the bridge. There is some uncertainty, although it could have been commenced by the former and finalised by the latter. However, the earliest textual evidence is by Sir Alexander Hay within the 1605 charter, which stated that the bridge was ordered and financed by Robert the Bruce. Its construction began in the late 13th century by Richard Cementarius, the famous mason, although the bridge was not finished until 1320. It had begun to deteriorate by the middle of the 16th century, but was extensively renovated by 1605.

By 1831 a newer bridge had been erected 1600 feet downstream from the Brig o' Balgownie. Today, the latter is called 'The Bridge of Don' and was built from the plans of Thomas Telford. It is also a fine construction. Each of its five semicircular granite arches has a span of 85 feet, its height is 38 feet above sea level and its parapets are twenty feet wide.

Throughout its history the Brig o' Balgownie has provided important service. For five centuries large armies have been able to move along the eastern coast and it has served various trade routes. The construction is of granite and sandstone. It has a single Gothic arch of over 39 feet. At low tide the top of the arch is located 55 feet above the waterline. Today, only pedestrians and cyclists may use the bridge. Its arch height is 32 feet, its span 60 feet and its carriageway is just 7 feet wide.

The origin of the word 'balgownie' is uncertain. The first part may come from baile or town. However, some earlier records regarding the Barony of Balgownie adopt the word palgoueny, or polgowny, or other extractions of *pol*. Pol associates with the word pool, and there is a pool near the bridge called the 'Black Neuk'. The river is about 20 feet deep at low tide, and the pool, 'Black Nook', on north side, is about 30 feet deep. Possible suggestions for the rest of the word, 'gownie', point to *gabhainn*, to suggest a cattle-fold, or gobhainn, which means a blacksmith.

Many other crossings could be mentioned in this account, but we must end that particular journey here. However, it is hoped that the general point will be apparent, that a great variety and frequency of river crossings have obtained in this landscape to accommodate the natural barriers of the Dee and Don. These powerful rivers result from many other dynamic watercourses and this will be explored forthwith.

THE ISLAND

School holidays. On fine days a bunch of us would walk to the River Dee. After crossing the King George VI Bridge, we'd scramble down the embankment and on to the path that ran between the field of corn and the river, chattering along it till we reached The Island.

It was an island at high tide only. Further along the path, a little bridge of land connected riverbank and island at low tide. There was a choice then. Some would walk on, to cross by dry land. The rest would paddle across and 'get their first'. We'd grasp grass in both hands and tie it at the top, again and again, forming a sun-dappled tunnel into which we crawled. Here we chatted on, breathing in the smell of Sweet Cicely. Sooner or later, the talk would come round to that part of the river that flowed under the bridge – of the bottomless pool there, and the conger eel that waited for the unwary. So any boy who'd brought a home-made fishing rod would cast his line close by.

Sometimes we would paddle in the shallows, looking for coloured pebbles in the clear water. And then there were the hunters, who would range from one end of the island to the other, on the look-out for big game, crashing past the multiple heads of the bright yellow Hawkbit, and heedless of the vetch that glowed purple from deep in the long grass. Heedless, too, of the admonitions of the fishermen that they would 'frighten the fish away'.

There was no need for watches, which was just as well, for none of us had one. Lengthening shadows, a coolness in the air, and an emptiness in the stomach sent us back the way we had come, leaving The Island silent and alone, until next time.

MARTHA BOTTRELL

RIVER DEE –
From the Old Invercauld Bridge
(after a storm)

Yesterday, the easy majesty of the powerful,
a great arc slowing in its own friction
regaled in purple finery, strutting its stuff,
showing its medals, an imperial procession
checked and balanced, ritually enframed
from the bridge. Today, below that bridge
that surely can take no more, trembling under
assault, a demented cry from the wilderness
beyond our knowing, engulfing the bank
transfixing those who are there to hear,
drifting through the pines like a benificence
to adoring trees attuned to its wild cry,
spiralling upwards into the great arenas of
the Stuic like rolling thunder to linger barely
diminished, then out, rising and falling
in exultation, the myriad falls drowned
in one final white throated roar, a spinning
vortex trailing in its wake attempting
equilibrium; a vast symphony headed for
the sea; music salmon come home to.

BRIAN LAWRIE

RIVER CROSSING

Blackly sinuous, the Dee snakes
Glinting eyes in the shredded moonlight,
Clouds race sea-ward like the river,
Muscular, pulling, drawing him
Into its depths.

He watches, desperate, in the darkness
It hints at amnesia, a blissful forgetting
A loss of self with its lonely failures,
To an ocean, bigger, deeper,
Drops united.

Family Christmas presents are wrapped
Early, left on friends' doorstep, safe
Should the river's cold embrace
Be his last

The wind pulls at striped pyjamas
And legs shake, he shudders,
At the coldness of it all.

Bridge darkens the depths,
Hinting at other roads
Car lights flicker and move on

His shadow stretched across the bridge,
Swings sideways and disappears
As he falters, uncertain,
Hovers between his tired worn existence and
The black cold solution tempting him
Never to return,
               'though still he may.

FRAN MARQUIS-FAULKES

THE ABERDEEN FERRY BOAT DISASTER

"Come awa Jessie. If ye dinna get a move on ye'll miss the ferry."

The foreman, standing at the door of the envelope works, pocket watch in hand, had to shout above the din of the machines.

"Ah'm coming" Mr. Galbraith.

A pretty young girl appeared, hastily fastening her coat ,but there was no need of a coat on this April day which was unusually warm.

"Off ye go then and mind ye've tae be back here wi' the mail fae Aiberdeen afore fower o'clock. And dinna bather gyan in aboot the Fair either. I ken near a'body's on holiday the day, but we're nae and we've jist tae buckle doon."

Jessie hurried down to the ferry station and was surprised to see a large crowd on the Aberdeen side, waiting to come to Torry. Of course, it was a Feast Day, the Fair was a great attraction and the public houses would do a roaring trade today.

It was nearly 3 in the afternoon, and the ferry was beginning to fill up. On board, Jessie saw Mrs.Craig, a friend of her mother, who had an empty creel on her back and went over to her.

"Hello Jessie. Hiv ye been running – ye've got pink cheeks.?"

"Aye, ah wis feart ah wis gonny miss the ferry, because ah've strict instructions to be back to the works wi' the mail afore fower."

"Oh aye, Mr. Galbraith's a hard taskmaster ah've heard, bit ye've plenty time. The water's gey roch the day though. I tak the ferry lots o' days bit I hivna seen it like this for a lang time. Mind you, there's been an affa rain this while, and wi' this mild wither, the sna on the hills would have melted and run doon intae the Dee."

As the ferry reached the Aberdeen side of the Dee, there were queues, orderly enough at first, but people became impatient and pushed their way onto the boat before those already on board, try as they might, had a chance to disembark.

"A'll niver get back in time wi' the mail noo, and a'll be in sic trouble wi' Mr. Galbraith."

Jessie was almost in tears.

"Hing oan tae ma creel, Jessie, or ye'll be ca'ed ower in the rush, a wee thing like you. Dinna worry aboot Mr. Galbraith. A'll hae a wird wi' him."

Jessie did as she was bid and the ferry was soon on its way back to the Torry side of the river. There were over 70 people now on a boat that was built to carry 40. It was operated on a pulley system attached by a wire rope at each end to either bank of the river and there was no engine, sails or rudder for guidance.

As they reached midstream the wire suddenly lifted clear of the water so that the rope from shore to shore formed an arc. The boat listed badly and the horrified watchers on the Torry side rushed to slacken the rope. Some of the passengers, sensing danger at this point, jumped into the water just before the boat capsized.

Mrs. Craig's husband had been on the river bank waiting for his wife and foreseeing the danger immediately launched a small boat. Encumbered by her creel and nearly strangled as well as drowned as she was seized on by others struggling to keep afloat, she was rescued by her husband and looked around desperately for Jessie, but there was no sign of her. Some of the people had managed to swim ashore, but the water was full of struggling screaming people, young and old.

A number of other boats, including a ferry manned by oarsmen was launched. Despite their efforts, of those who had been on board, only 44 were saved. In the days following, prolonged searches were made in the vicinity and in the harbour with little success, and it seemed that a number had been swept out to sea. Several were later found in the irrigation channel.

The disaster had occurred on 5th April, 1876, and at the ensuing Court of Enquiry it was established that the wire rope had been replaced some time previous to the accident but not sufficient wire had been bought and a length had had to be added. It was possible that the splicing had not been well done and the rope had in fact broken. Statements were taken from many who had witnessed the accident, and it was noted particularly that the ferryman, William Masson, had been heard to say that the boat could go if it liked but he was certainly not going on it. He had been in the job only 2 months, and was seen to have words with the man who leased the boat from the Town Council, namely Alexander Kennedy, about the number of passengers being allowed on board, but Mr. Kennedy denied that any such conversation took place.

After the disaster door-to-door collections were arranged and generous contributions were made by the townspeople to aid the survivors and the families of those who were lost, poems were written and sold to add to the fund and the Town Council and Harbour Commissioners also contributed. There had been discussions by the Councillors for a long time that a bridge should be built over the Dee and there is no doubt that the disaster hastened the building of the Queen Victoria Bridge, which was finally opened on July 2nd 1881. It was partly funded by public subscription and partly by Aberdeen Corporation.

A plaque commemorating the disaster and those who lost their lives was erected on the bridge and on February 6th, 2005 this was unveiled by Kate Dean, leader of Aberdeen City Council. Pupils from Walker Road school, dressed in Victorian style, marched over the bridge preceded by the Town Drummer. A Salvation Army band played while the onlookers sang the seamen's hymn 'Eternal Father Strong to Save'.

This was a fitting memorial to those who lost their lives on that dreadful April day in 1876.

ANN NICOL

MICHAEL PEGLER

Old Bridge of Dee, Invercauld

BILL ANDERSON

Slow Walk

Fran Marquis-Faulkes

Michael Pegler

Cambus o' May Suspension Bridge
William Hume

Chapter 5

Tributaries along the way

A coalition of waterways forms greater currents in the lower valleys of major rivers. Their singular features and collective destinations identify such tributaries. The term 'tributary' comes from a Middle English word *tributarie* that is ultimately retrievable from the Latin, tribuere, 'divide between tribes'. Various streams and rivers serve the Dee and Don, and the latter are also two 'tribes' of the North Sea.

To where will these tributaries lead us in this account? The sources of some tributaries, their topographical features and, occasionally, their proximity to townships will be described. Occasionally there will be a mention of significant events, structures or sites where these have been ignored in other chapters. However, the main purpose is to express the extent of tributary water that supplies the Dee and Don, from where they are drawn and their orientation west to east along each valley. Throughout this account the terms 'left' or 'right' will be adopted in accordance with a convention that assumes a perspective that faces downstream in every case.

The chief tributaries of the Don are Conrie Water, Ernan Water, the Water of Carvie, the Water of Nochty, Deskry Water, the Water of Buchat, Kindy Burn, Mossat Burn, Leochel Burn and the River Urie. There are many other streams that ultimately add to the Don's course.

The Don first draws from such streams as *Feith Bhait*, *Meoir Veannaich* and *Allt nan Aighean*. Alex Inkson McConnochie notes that the very first rise of the Don occurs in *Coire Dhomhain*, which means 'deep corrie'. It is at the bottom of the latter among a level area of heath and rush that a modest fall of water occurs at the head of *Allt an Mhicheil*, translated from the Scottish

Gaelic as Michael's Burn. However, on occasion this source is thought to overflow to the Avon valley.

From such points of elevation, north of the young river, as *Druim Bhurich*, *Cairn Vaich* and *Carn Meadhonach* are drawn *Feith Bhait*, *Allt Reppachie*, Tallin Burn and the burn of Loinherry. From such points of elevation south of the young river can be noted *Carn Culchavie*, from which *Culchavie Burn* flows into the right bank from the *Coire Culchavie*. *Meoir Veannaich* draws from the elevations of *Coire Dhomhain* and *Torran Deallaig*. Duiveoir Burn runs from The Leitir. Liana Burn *Bruach Ruadh* and *Allt Bad a' Chuirn* runs from Badochurch and *Allt a' Choilich*, or Cock Burn runs from *Tom a' Gharaidh*.

The burn of Loinherry draws from three springs and almost retains a constant width throughout its course. The most easterly stream of these three, lies close to The Lecht road and the county borders on the eastern slope of *Carn Mhic an Toisich*. There is a disused iron mine in the vicinity, on the right bank (1930 feet). The latter stopped production in 1866 because the prevailing haulage cost affected its commercial viability. The area is rich in iron ore, which is also found near the head of Glen Ernan and Glen Nochty near the ridge *Leac a' Ghobhainn*. The Cock Burn, derives its name from a hamlet, The Cock, situated in upper Strathdon. Cock Burn starts between Brown Cow Hill and Camock Hill (2200 feet) and enters the Don downstream from the Loinherry, on the right bank.

North of Deeside's Ballater stretches the major uplands of Morven, the general area from which the Conrie and Carvie waters begin their descent to Donside. Conrie starts as *Allt Fuaranach* from Cairnlea Hill below *Tom a' Bhùraich* (1840 feet) and it is joined on its right bank by waters draining from the elevation of *Scraulac*. The latter runs past Cairnagour Hill on its right and Little Scraulac on its left. The Conrie eventually flows through a landscape enhanced by tracts of pine forest, such as those near the settlement of Fleuchats below Gallow Hill (1460 feet), until it enters the Don's right bank at Culfork just upstream from the Ernan, opposite Lonach Hill.

The Water of Carvie rises among the steep contours of *Blàdubh* below the rocky Slacks of Glencarvie, *Cairn Mona Gowan* (2600 feet) and *Mullachdubh* (2230 feet). It runs north, draining water from *Meikle Charsk* (1925 feet) on its left. For a time there are tracts of pine forest along the steep slopes of the valley, which then opens out as the Carvie flows through Birkford. Its course continues between *Cnocna h-Iolaire* below *Craig of Bunzeach* (1740 feet) on the right and Gallows Hill (1430 feet) on the left. The tributary continues through the Mains of Glencarvie to join the River Don opposite Candacraig House.

Ernan Water emerges amid the hills of *Meikle Corr Riabhach* (2540 feet) and Carn Liath (2550 feet). Its course continues for 7 miles in an easterly direction until it meets the Don's left bank at Inverernan. During the latter journey, Ernan Water will have descended 1290 feet . The west of Glen Ernan faces the Edinglassie Estate near Huntly, opposite Carn Mor. The lower part of Carn Mor constitutes Lonarch Hill, which is circumscribed by the Don and mentioned in the first chapter. In some respects the Ernan valley is a wilder prospect than that of Glen Buckat and Nochty, although they rise in close company to each other, in the general area of the Ladder Hills.

The Water of Nochty is initially fed by three burns: The burn of *Allt Slochd Chaimbeil* runs from beneath the elevation of Carn Liath (2590 feet) passing the *Monadh Slochd Chaimbeil*. The burn of the *Allt ant-Sluichd Mhoir* runs from beneath Carn Mor (2630 feet) past Broom Knowe (2260 feet) on its left, while draining another rivulet from between *Monadh an t-Sluich Leith* and *Monadh Slochd Chaimbeil* to its right. Lastly the burn of *Allt na Caillich* runs from beneath Dun Muir (2470 feet) between Broom Knowe (2260 feet) on its right and Finlate Hill (2020 feet) on its left. This growing tribe is joined by Little Burn near a place called Duffdefiance, beneath the Hill of Aldachuie. Quillichan Burn from Dubh Breac Hill (1190 feet) enters the right bank of the Nochty. Passing the ruin of Corrie Breck, the Nochty then flows past forests and the settlement of Torrancroy below Ladylea Hill (1990 feet) to its north and the heights of Moss Hill (2100 feet). From here the Nochty enters the left bank of the Don near Bellabeg. At this point the Water of Nochty, crossed by the A944 road, is near the Doune of Invernochty and a fine church granted by the Earl of Mar.

Deskry Water originates south of Strathdon on the slopes of Morven (2850 feet). Passing the craggy summit of *Preas Whin*, on its right, the embryonic stream of *Allt Devanach* runs north, drawing water from the Braes of Fintock from the west. After Corbies Nest it flows below Ardan Breac hill to its right and *Bad an Teachdaire* to its left. Its course extends 9 miles in a north-eastwardly direction, flowing past the Forest of Bunzeach and Craig of Bunzeach (1450 feet). After Badnagoach, the burn of Badaseaneach joins the Deskry. The stream will have passed the Hill of Bogston, Hillockhead, the Boultenstone Outdoor Centre and Foggie Mill. It is joined by the Tomdubh Burn, which runs from the lochs below Tom Dubh and travels under a bridge past Broom Hill and Blue Mill before its course describes an excessively sharp turn to join the River Don at is right bank. The Deskryshiel Lodge, situated near here at the Deskry Water, is found at the base of Birk Hill.

The Water of Buchat is created at the juncture of two burns below *Allt Badaneoin*. These tributary streams arise in the west, in the case of Coulins Burn, which seeps from Geal Charn (2240 feet) and the east, in the case of Leadensider Burn, which derives from a small tarn near the top of Crespet Hill (1820 feet).

The Don is still quite shallow and follows a turbulent course across a rocky bed while the Mossat Burn, joining on the left bank, runs a slothful course in its upper reaches, passing close to the A944 road. The Mossat Burn runs past 'Little Wood' in Littlewood Park. Along its course occurs the Craigs of Logie (1160 feet), a wooded elevation on Brux Hill (1560 feet), to its right. In the vicinity is the renowned 'Nine Maidens' Well'. An explanation of the latter name is recounted in our eighth chapter.

Ten *eirde* houses, earth houses or souterrains, have been located near here. The specific area is between Drumnahive Wood and Mossat Burn. Subterranean villages or possibly towns are suggested by this discovery. Eirde houses usually offer no sign above ground, apart from a very small entrance. The latter leads down a gradient of six feet into a low chamber where it may be just possible to stand. Twenty feet long with other rooms left and right, the chambers are about eight feet wide at the stone floor. However, the progressive overlapping of the stone walls converge to six feet across the breadth of the top.

Tuach Burn runs near the Chapel of Hallforest and Hallforest Castle, about a mile south of Kintore. Adjoining Kintore to the west is 'Deer Den', an ancient Roman camp. Dividing the road and railway it enters the town from the south. Tuach Hill (278 feet) is almost encircled by the Tuach Burn as it winds its way towards the Don. On nearby Gallow Top there are the remnants of a stone circle called 'The Kings Seat'.

Hangman's Croft is at other end of town east of Bridgeales House.

The River Urie is a small river situated in the Garioch, said to be good for trout fishing, and its main tributary is the Gadie Burn. Its origins are close to Bennachie, approximately 25 miles to the north-west of Aberdeen. It rises to the south of Largie, 4½ miles south-south-east of Huntly. It progresses to the south-east for 20 miles. Along the way it passes such settlements and parishes as Gartly, Drumblade, Insch, Forgue, Culsalmond, Oyne, Rayne, Chapel-of-Garioch, Keithhall, Pitcaple and Milton of Inveramsay. The Urie eventually joins the Don just downstream of Inverurie.

Before leaving our exploration of the Don's tributaries we could mention the Goval Burn, which drains from Loch Goval. The latter name is derived from the Gaelic, Goull. In earlier times, the tributary is said to have been sufficient to turn several corn mills during the course of its run. The loch is commonly known as 'Bishops Loch', for it transpired that the Bishops of Aberdeen occupied a palace on the island of the loch. The latter had a draw-bridge connecting it to the land. The Goval Burn flows to the south, joining the Don's left bank near the Bridge of Dyce.

The first tributary of the Dee is the water from the pools of Dee, *Lochan Dubh na Lairige* which means 'black tarn' or 'tarns of the hill past', referring to the pools being farther back into the Lairig Ghru. The Tailor's Burn or *Allt Clach Nan Taillear*, joins the Dee after its rise on Ben Macdhui and subsequent journey out of the corrie of the same name, *Choire Clach Nan Taillear*. A tragedy in that area is marked by a collection of stones farther downstream, near the footpath. This is where three tailors met their demise in the harsh conditions of the snow-laden uplands. They were attempting to dance in the three dales of Abernethy, Rothiemurchus and Dalmore in Mar. Their ambition was to do all three dances within 24 hours, but it would seem that by the last dale they were overcome by exhaustion.

The river flows over the Chest of Dee on its way to White Bridge and its rendezvous with the Geldie Burn. The Lui Water enters the Dee on the left bank after the Linn of Dee. Both the burns of Luibeg and Derry feed the former.

As one of these streams runs through Glen Luibeg, high in the Cairngorms it draws from Lochan Uaine and Coure Stan Dearg. The stream drains from various waters between Carn a Mhaim and Sron Riach. The Derry Burn draws water from many sources including the impressive Loch Etchachan in the Cairngorms below the steep edifice that sits above Coire Etchachan. Lochan Uaine (or 'Green Tarn'), is much smaller and is situated south-west of the latter near Cairn Toul.

The Quoich Water also joins the growing River Dee. It rises east of the corries of Beinn a' Bhuird below the elevations of North Top (3920 feet) and South Top (3860 feet) from where it is supplied with the waters of various tarns. *Clach a' Cleirich* (Stone of Priest) stands near the end of an ancient footpath traced from *Gleann an t Slagain* towards two burns, *Alltt an Duish Lochan* and *Glas Allt Mor*, which add to Quoich Water. They flow through forests of Caledonian Pine, joining the Dubh Glinne, a burn that draws from *Dubh Ghleann* or Black Glen. The Quoich water passes under a wooden road bridge. Above this is a footbridge across a natural bowl in the river, which is called the Earl of Mar's Punch Bowl. The folklore asserts that it was the site of hunt celebrations, wherein whiskey, honey and boiling water was added to cheer the present company.

Clunie Water and Callater Burn conjoin at Braemar. Clunie Water draws from tributary burns on the Cairnwell Pass, incorporating the corries and elevations of *Coire Fionn*, *Garbh Cohoire* and *Cairn of Claise*. There are other tributaries that seep from the Baddoch, including Callater Burn from Glen Callater and, in turn, Loch Callater and the *Choire Loch Kander*.

There is a royal retreat at the shiel of Auchtavan, the last dwelling high in the isolated Glen Feardar. The Feardar Burn that courses through the latter glen joins the Dee's left bank among the forests surrounding the settlement of Inver just west of Crathie; standing at an altitude of 1498 feet with fine views of Lochnagar mountain.

The Rivers Muick and Gairn join the Dee at Ballater. The River Gairn is the longest tributary of the River Dee. It is over 20 miles long and though the last 5 miles of its course from Gairnshiel to the Dee is well known it rises in one of the most remote parts of the Cairngorms. From modest pools among peat and heather it runs down the grassy levels above Glen Gairn. The twisting bends in its early reaches incorporate clear pools around its source where there is a stone *Na Clach Reachdan* ('Stone of the Statute') that is possibly a marker of some previous dispute.

The Gairn flows through the precipitous hills of *Craig an Dail Mhor* and

Craig a Dail Beag. To the north occurs Ben Avon, characterised by an abundance of granite tors surmounting its plateau. Several burns flow from its south side such as *Allt an Eas Mhoir*, 'the burn of the big waterfall', or *Muckle Easaidh*. The latter joins the Gairn among several old shielings, proceeding through grass, heather and boulders. There is a tor upon Ben Avon called *Clach Bhan*, its geological configuration having formed places to sit. There are also pools gouged from the granite by natural erosion. Folklore tells us that women came here from far away having faith in the benefits of sitting here, believing that it could ease the pain of childbirth. There are more stories associated with the *Muckle Easaidh* that recount the discovery of a headless body between Loch Builg and Corndavon Lodge. There are a few small shielings west of Shenalt Burn and a ruin called Ruighe Baille from *Ruighe Baille a' Chlagain* (*ruighe* means shiel), which was the shiel of *Ballachlaggan*.

Downstream occurs Dorndavon Lodge where Brown Cow Hill features in the skyline on the left bank of the Gairn. Occasionally there is a lingering snow patch called the 'The White Calf Hill', from *A' Bho Dhonn*. Nearby lies the Delnabo ruin, which once was Daldownie Farm. Past the settlement of Daldownie, the Duchrie Burn flows into Gairn. There is a pool in the Gairn by the side of the public road called the *Sgeir an Deoc*.

The River Muick flows out of Loch Muick and joins the Dee close to Ballater. Its burns and lochs draw water from the hills above. Lochnagar is clearly seen, and on its slopes a huge skull with antlers known as the 'Stag Horn Wreath' sometimes appears, formed by the natural configuration of the melting snow.

Loch Muick is very deep, possibly 239 feet. Legend has it that the loch was once crossed on foot. One winter when all was frozen, a young boy crested the hill and saw the lights of *Glas Allt* from the top of the ancient pass of Chapel Mounth. To ensure his safe journey home he headed straight towards the lights and reached home accordingly. In the morning his noctural tracks were still preserved on the surface of the frozen ground and indicated that he had walked across the loch!

The Aven and Dye join the Water of Feugh before the riverside fields of Strachan are reached. From here the Feugh continues to join the River Dee at Banchory. The Feugh is 20 miles long, rising on the hills of Cammie on the Aberdeenshire and Angus border from where it flows into the Forest of Birse. The Dye draws its waters from the Hill of Edendocher, the Hill of Fingray (1590 feet), Clachnaben (1930 feet) and Cairn o' Mount (1490 feet). Clochnaben is an easily identified elevation for at its top obtains a massive singular rock measuring 95 feet.

With the addition of the Water of Charr, the course of the Dye goes under the Bridge of Dye, built by Sir Alexander Fraser in 1691. This valley is host to the Cairn a' Mounth, now the line of the B974. Macbeth and Edward I used this Deeside entrance, as mentioned in the second chapter. The Dye's lower reaches pass the Bridge of Bogendreip and on through pine forests where it meets the Water of Feugh near Strachan. Stachan's outlook is graced by four predominant hills: Clochnaben, as mentioned above; Mount Battock (2550 feet); Kerloch (1744 feet) and Mount Shade (1660 feet).

By now it must be plain to see that the frequency of watercourses that populate the 'tribes' of the Dee and Don are innumerable. The exchanges within the catchment areas of the Dee and Don lead us to consider other systems of dependent exchanges, such as the giving and taking of life that functions between creatures. The chapter that follows explores aspects of the latter as well as the actions of human beings charged with the management of precious environments and the organic life they contain.

FAR THE CORBIE RINS

A tributary of the River Dee
Runs through a deep ravine
Where there has been, in days of old,
Hidden – a pot of gold.
The tenants there of this had heard,
And they implored their Aberdonian Laird
To let them dam the waterfall,
As all that water hid this treasure
Through caverns beyond measure –
"Caverns measureless to man…"
The Laird said, "Yes – you can.
But there's a kelpie in the gully
Who guards that pot of gold…
You must be brisk and bold!"
Nothing daunted
All the tenants made
Blocks with rocks
To dam the waterfall…
They watched the water run away –
But suddenly –
As they began to wade –
An eerie voice did say:
"The hoose is on fire!
The hoose is on fire!"
The tenants were afraid;
They stopped their search,
And climbed the cliffs to see
Kincoosie hoose on fire indeed,
And, by the time they did succeed
To quench the flames – Ah! then –
The dam had broken,
And water hid the pot of gold again
Because it was the kelpie who had spoken.

VALERIE IRVINE-FORTESCUE

TURBULENT TRIBUTARY

Running o'er the heather, desperate to swim,
Looking at the gorge, cool waters below,
Leaping hand in hand into the blue flow,
Yelping with joy in the beautiful Linn.
Splishing and splashing and wearing a grin,
Fighting the current, determined to show,
Her skill in keeping the water below,
Never wanting the water her chagrin.
But, the currents alive – under the rocks,
Pushing and pulling, and holding under,
Grabbing all her strength – the noise like thunder,
And then nothing. Still. The secret unlocks.
Seen from the top – a work of abstract art
A crafted creation of death and dark.

RICKY ROBB

A feast near the source of the Dee

BILL ANDERSON

Michael Pegler

A youthful Don

Norman Thomson

Dee and Don – Inspiration

Water of Feugh, Banchory

Michael Pegler

Chapter 6

Hunting and the Hunted

The natural world embodies a system of predation between complex chains of biological organisms wherein the hunter at some point must be hunted. Conceptions of this natural world have motivated imagination from the very first moments of human existence, as exemplified in early cave painting. Indeed, human awareness of mortality, that death stalks us all, has inspired a host of moral and ethical belief systems.

If we unpack the term 'hunting' we reveal other notions. The purpose of the predatory aspect of the hunter may entail the need for food or, in some human accounts, various notions of sport. The latter may be bound up with the former within a tradition of necessary management where it is crucial to protect the livestock of farmers or bring about controls over other negative effects of a particular species that are designated the status of pest.

With this in mind, it should be noted that such notions of pursuit, as obtained from the term 'hunting', also require unpacking. For one thing, it is possible to pursue either directly or indirectly, in the sense of bringing about a necessary objective. In the former version of hunting the quarry is chased down until caught and killed. In the latter, the predator lies in wait or creeps stealthily upon its prey. When the predator is human, it is often the case that the kill can be made while still some distance away from the target. Therefore, a distinction obtains between the general notion of hunting and this latter notion of stalking. The control of deer populations, for example, entails deerstalking in Scotland because hunting with hounds to control foxes or deer has been illegal for some time. Those species that are regularly stalked are broadly termed 'game', whether fish, bird or mammal.

Red grouse, *lagopus lagopus scoticus*, is a subspecies of the willow grouse, *lagopus lagopus*. The latter may be called the willow ptarmigan in North America. However, the red grouse is distinguished from the latter in that it does not grow white plumage during the winter season.

The red grouse is a medium-sized game bird with a corpulent body, short tail and a slight curvature of the bill. As its name suggests, its colour is a reddish-brown with ashen coloured feathers on legs and feet. Its breeding environment is the uplands and it is a permanent resident of the British Isles. The extent of its travel is limited and reasons for its decline are either disease or reduction of habitat. Grouse breed among heather moorland, often frequenting upland bogs, rough grazing and coastal heaths or spending winter seasons nearer farmland in order to find nutrition during heavy snow cover. It is seen most readily on heather moors if surprised or agitated from its cover, thus causing it to suddenly fly upwards. Its flight entails a rapid buzzing of the wings. Grouse feed on the heather, seeds, berries and any insects found. The sound that red grouse make has usually been described as 'go-back, go-back, go-back'.

Although pheasant, partridge and duck are considered game, the indigenous red grouse will feature as the game bird of this account. Estates are divided into beats with the average estate having about five gamekeepers. Normally there are about four to eight guns set for the shoot, behind butts, towards which the beaters 'walk up' and 'flush out' the grouse with two dogs. As the birds launch into the air they are driven towards the standing guns and are shot accordingly.

Since the 19th century, grouse shooting features significantly in the estate activity and as an important financial resource. A few grouse could be taken sustainedly from unmanaged moorland, but taking larger numbers entails several land management strategies. These include the supervision of heather habitat using a controlled burning known as *muirburn*, as well as allowing limited grazing. In addition, predator and disease controls are essential given that grouse are managed in their natural environment.

There is judged to be a British stock of 250,000 pairs of grouse. It is possible to have 50 pairs per square kilometre in the breeding season. Populations of grouse have decreased in Scotland causing the red grouse to be of greater concern in terms of conservation. Various contributory factors have brought about this state of affairs. Grouse appear to thrive better in areas where a ground cover of 40 per cent to 80 per cent of nutrient-rich heather obtains. However, nationally there is just 30 per cent of such moorland as a result of past overgrazing by deer and sheep during the winter seasons. Also much of this environment has been previously lost to forestry and a decline in the controlled heather burns that used to promote new growth. Grouse populations are also vulnerable to increased predation and instances of reduced gamekeeper operations or inappropriate land management.

Disease and parasites can also seriously affect grouse populations. Louping ill, a virus transmitted to the grouse by sheep ticks, can limit chick survival by 80 per cent. Although regular sheep dipping can ameliorate the frequency of tick bites upon red grouse this is obviously an insufficient strategy if deer or mountain hare are tick carriers. Other parasites such as the nematode worm, *trichostrongylus tenuis*, infect grouse with strongylosis, hence reproduction is hampered and death can result.

It is argued that there is an integrated benefit in maintaining heather-dominated habitats for various species, and that humans also benefit in the creation of rural employment and income resulting from such grouse moor conservation. Sustaining grouse density entails controlling predators, limiting disease and heather management. Many people observe a desire to see this range of species restored through policies that encourage the provision of driven grouse shooting because of the associated benefits for heather moorland.

Game fishing in the Dee and Don includes salmon, sea trout and brown trout. The mature salmon are silver with spotted flanks. Males have red spots and a pink hue to their underside during the breeding season while their lower jaw extends into a hooked form. The dimensions of the largest of these beautiful fish can be 5 feet in length and over 70 lbs in weight.

The first two years or more of a salmon's life is spent in the river whereupon it swims to the sea to feed near Greenland, remaining there for one or two years more. It returns to the same river from where it originated, in order to spawn. It is thought its directional ability entails recognition of the taste of its home river. Some repeat this process, but normally the life span is limited to three to five years.

Spawning occurs in the upper reaches of watercourses in late October or early February. The female uses its tail to scoop a hollow, or *redd*, in the river gravel. She lays 2,000 to 15,000 eggs in this hollow and forms another upstream, thereby covering the eggs in the former. The adult salmon are exhausted after spawning and many die. Some survivors continue to exist in the river during the winter or float downstream to the sea.

The eggs hatch in March to April and leave the gravel when they become *fry*, only a few inches long. The fry eat larvae and very small water animals. By one to three years they are referred to as *parr* and have dark markings on their body, which help to disguise them. After the spring of the third or fourth year they become known as *smolt*, about six inches long, their fins becoming black and their body silver. They swim to the estuary eating shrimps and other estuarial fish. Having adapted to the salt water they leave for the sea where they eat a wide range of fish and plankton, and grow much faster as a result. Upon their return to spawn they must navigate waterfalls and other obstacles over which they may jump as high as ten feet. The salmon fly-fishing season on the Dee runs from 1st February until 30th September, and any more than seven fish caught on the Dee must be released. Fishing in the Don has greatly improved since the closure of the paper mills. On the Don the season runs from 11th February until 31st October.

Six species of deer live wild in the British Isles: red; roe; muntjac; fallow; sika and, less commonly, the Chinese water deer. Only the red, *cervus elaphus*, and the roe, *capreolus capreolus*, are indigenous. The following refers to the subspecies of red deer in Scotland, *cervus elaphus scoticus*.

Red deer have existed for more than twelve million years. The accessibility afforded by the ice age explains the wide distribution of this species. Its success is associated with the hunting of predators such as bear, lynx and wolf. Mankind's hunting practices have also served the survival of the deer species in the 17th and 18th centuries when the deer were under royal protection.

Red deer are natural woodland creatures forced by prevailing circumstances to adapt to moorland environments. As a result of the poorer nutrition on moorland, deer specimens are smaller than those able to live in the woodlands. A red deer is a dark red or brown colour in summer with cream underbelly, inner thighs and rump. Sometimes spots may be discerned on these summer coats, especially along the back. The coat changes to a darker brown or grey in winter with lighter patches on the rump and undersides. There is a visible gland high on the cannon bones of the rear legs, immediately above the hoof. Age and condition alter appearance, older deer fading to ginger in colour. Red deer can trot and swim long distances. They can live to 20 years, but rarely beyond fifteen. Most deaths are during the first week, this vulnerability being contingent upon the weather and predation by foxes or golden eagles, which take newborn calves. Death in old age is contingent upon the capacity to eat, and hence tooth wear is a major factor.

A rise in testosterone levels prior to the mating season signals certain physical changes and prompts associated activities in the *rut*. A stag's neck thickens and a mane develops. All deer species, including red deer, have several external glands to mark areas, to signal readiness for mating and possibly to assist in recognition between individuals. There are glands below the eyes, reproductive organs, lower back, legs and between hoof cleavage. Deer hinds breed from three to 13 years of age and stags mate from five to 11 years of age.

The ratio of light to dark hours in the day affects the life cycle of deer. Testosterone also instigates the cleaning of velvet from the antlers. Intolerance ensues between stags that have been previously living alongside each other. Hinds congregate in early September and stags gather their hinds. The stags must then defend that territory. Mature stags lose condition, and weight drops by one fifth over the six weeks of the rutting period, which peaks by the middle of October.

Stag fights can cause serious or fatal injuries. Stags roar their status and bark warning to younger stags. The scent marking of territories occurs, called *thrashing and wiping*. Other activity includes wallowing in muddy pools laced with their urine. Mutual sniffing and licking between hinds and stags takes place. Stags pursue, or *chivy* hinds with neck and tongue extended. The gestation period of red deer is about eight months. At about 12 lbs, calves are born from late May, but usually early to mid-June. Calves have a shorter head, having fewer teeth, and have pale spots on their coats from birth until about two months.

External parasites of deer include ticks, keds and lice. Nasal botfly and warble fly cause a great deal of suffering. The castor bean tick may carry

Lyme disease, which may affect humans where symptoms are left untreated. There are internal parasites in deer that include liver fluke, lungworm and nematode. Although causing discomfort, these parasites seldom prove fatal. Very rarely, notifiable diseases such as tuberculosis, foot-and-mouth and anthrax infect deer.

Antler growth relates to nutrition. There is a difference between the growth of highland and lowland deer antlers. The former have 12 points, *tines*, while the lowland deer antlers have more tines that are also heavier. As testosterone decreases, antlers detach from mid-March and through April. Deer may chew fallen antlers to redress calcium deficiency. New growth is clothed in velvet, which is very sensitised, seething with blood to form bone tissue. Conflict at this time entails boxing with the deer's front feet in protection of the sensitive antlers. By July, the blood supply to antlers ceases and the deer will rub the itching velvet until it has been removed.

The above process starts after the second year. The first year entails developing pedicles, bony protuberances that later carry the antlers. These become apparent in the first winter. By year two they are called a *knobber* or *brocket*. The *spiker* stage ensues in the third year. Thereafter, antlers increase in length, weight and the number of tines and points, until between years seven to nine when a full head of antlers obtain.

Abnormality may occur whether inherited through injury, illness or malnourishment. A *hummel* is a stag without antlers. Such deer are heavier because the nutrition normally supplied to antler growth is made available elsewhere. This condition is not hereditary and hummels can reproduce. A *switch* is a deer with antlers that are without tines or with just brow tines. This abnormality may be congenital or related to age. Sometimes switches are killers, for without tines their spikes will pass between the defensive entanglement that tines present during the rut.

Roe deer, *capreolus capreolus*, are relatively common and much smaller than red deer. Roe deer may have been native to Britain for 6,000 or even 10,000 years. Earlier habitat erosion and over-hunting threatened extinction by the year 1800, but improving conditions have meant roe deer are prevalent once more. Upon maturity they are about 55 lbs in weight and present about 25 inches at the shoulder. The males, *bucks*, are slightly larger than the females, *does*. Their colouring is also red during the summer, tending to grey during the winter. They have a black nose with white spots and chin. Both genders have a white area around the rump and are without a significant tail. Each antler is quite short with just three tines upon maturity. Their life span can extend to 16 years, but bucks often die before five years, and does before six or seven years. Death is very common in the winter season, during birth and immediately after birth.

The habitat of roe deer is normally along the margins of woodland, but occasionally they stray into fields. Food sources include tree shoots, brambles, ivy, heather, various herbs or cereals. Usually unaccompanied, roe deer tend to gather during the winter. The sound of the buck is a short bark with a harsher rasp during courtship, while the doe produces a high pitched call.

Roe bucks are territorial and aggressive during the rut. The rut itself takes place between mid-July and mid-August. Fighting among bucks often results in death or severe injury. Female deer are not territorial and have several home ranges that overlay one another. Bucks and does have more than one breeding partner. Giving birth between May and June, does over a year old could have one or two offspring, but rarely three. Uniquely in deer species the gestation period of roe deer includes a four-month period of embryonic suspended animation, *diapause*, with a subsequent five months of normal growth. This may be an adaptation to aid survival in harsh winters. The most active times of roe deer are at dawn and dusk. Roe spend a long time lying down between these feeding periods.

Eating tree shoots and agricultural crops damages the economic interests of some farmers and foresters, although country and forest estates gain revenue for deer stalking. Red deer are shot at particular times; stags from 7th July until 21st October and hinds 21st October until 14th February. Guest shooters can pay £350 to £500 to accompany a gamekeeper on a shoot or deer stalking trip, and must have the correct warranties, including a game license and firearm certificate in keeping with current legislation. However, with wholesale venison prices at 30 pence per lb the aim of shooting deer is no longer to supply food. The rationale is to control herd numbers in proportion to the resources of a land devoid of the deer's natural predators. Such culling improves the health of the herd, its capacity to survive harsh conditions and resists disease.

A traditional red deer stalking party consists of the gamekeeper, who will lead the party, often a guest shooter, a walking ghillie employed as a carrier of guns and other equipment and a pony ghillie, the latter usually being in charge of a sturdy Scottish horse called a *garron*. A 0.27 calibre, high velocity rifle is a popular calibre used to kill the deer. The target is just behind the front quarter, and the shot is taken over a distance of about 300 to 400 feet. After the kill the carcass is gutted, whereupon the intestines or *gralloch* are discarded, but the various organs, the *pluck*, are kept. The deer carcass is then carried on horseback equipped with a special deer saddle. Stalking a roe deer entails a different operation because that type of deer is usually found in woodland cover not open land. Stalking occurs at dawn and dusk between the times that the creature is resting.

There is a moral imperative that addresses the justification of any act of killing. The latter is a complex issue, for it entails a wide range of practical matters regarding the interspecies dependency of both flora and fauna, and includes the local economies of people.

There is a tension between a rationale based upon a moral imperative to manage the environment and one based upon a moral imperative to limit our negative impact upon it. A moment's reflection should reveal that within each case the other case is present. Our cognitive capacity to take an objective view regarding the patterns of interdependency in nature will mislead us if we forget to include ourselves within that picture. A balanced diversity in the environment remains possible where the organisms that constitute that biological system sustain each other through a chain of predation, with regard to which humanity is not exempt, for nature reclaims all her children.

The evolution of humanity from a hunter-gatherer existence includes movement towards an agricultural provision. Once settlements began to flourish, some security from natural predation obtained. These small communities will have developed into the hamlets and villages that mark a rich history. The latter also provides a suitable entrance to the next enquiry.

THE SALMON

Oh tae be a salmon, comin skelpin doon the Dee!
Simmer scalin ower ma tail,
Lowpin through the linns,
Wummlin ower the rapids, i' the cauld, snaw bree,
An jinkin aa the fishers wi ma fins.

I widna dauchle b' the banks,
Hob-nobbin wi the glegs,
Or coorie i' the puils abeen Braemar
I'd come breengin up oot-ower the whins
Like forty thoosan flegs;
Jist a skeely, skyty limmer,
Wi the shimmer o a star!

Syne, I'd turn aroon an up again
(I canna bide awa frae the bonnie watter
Birlin neth ma wame)
A salmon in its element, the heather an the faem,
A contermashious salmon winnin hame.

SHEENA BLACKHALL

THE LAST FIGHT

Up and down the river
I move.
Slowly,
Enticed.

In eager anticipation
I wait.
In the dark,
Patient.

A shimmering shape
I see.
Dancing,
Inviting.

Upwards to the light
I reach.
Engulfing,
My reward.

Pulled and pushed.
Light, dark,
Turmoil,
Panic.

Surrendering to the force
I stop.
Quiet,
Beaten.

Ricky Robb

Stag

JOHN MORGAN

Hunting trip

Ricky Thomas

Fishing on the river

TERRY FINCHER

Michael Pegler

Chapter 7

✦

Villages and Villagers

The history of a village extends its course to touch and be touched by many lives. Apart from being a category of settlement distinguished in terms of its physical extent or by its institutions, a village is also a subset of other general notions that co-ordinate names and landmarks with historical events. Such unique traces attach a memorable narrative that matures to establish the qualitative identity of each place.

Certain terms, which need mentioning, are used in framing the identity of the following places of this account. Today Scotland uses a unitary system of local authority that consists of 32 *council areas*, but before 1996 a system of two levels obtained, with the exception of three unitary island authorities. This consisted of nine regions divided into 53 districts. The latter replaced a system of 33 *county* administrations that were discontinued in 1974 and had replaced the old counties from 1889. Prior to this, villages were associated with certain ecclesiastical parishes that dated from the medieval period. Such quoad sacra parishes required parishioners to give part of their income to support the church authorities. By the 17th century taxation was governed in Scotland by *burghs*, *sheriffdoms* and *parishes*, as created by Royal Charter. From 1845 until 1860 civil or *quoad civilia* parishes were formed and the members of their committees were elected. The latter type of parish existed until 1975. In an altered sense these parishes still persist for registration purposes, but *quoad sacra* parishes are increasingly merged as congregations diminish.

The account that follows is organised in two sections to summarise a progression through some villages of Deeside and Donside while generally travelling west to east in each case. Given the space available, it is regrettable that there will be places of equal interest that must be overlooked. The first section of this account begins on upper Deeside.

The district of Braemar spans Clunie Water a mile before joining with the River Dee. It is comprised of Castleton village in the east and Auchendryne village in the west. As an ancient parish, Castleton of Braemar was linked to Crathie. It was originally called St Andrews, but was later named *Caenn-na-droehait*, signifying 'bridge-end'. As Queen Mary's reign ended, Castleton became the property of the Earl of Mar to become part of Braemar. Nearly central to Braemar can be found a stone cottage where, in 1881, Robert Louis Stevenson wrote most of the book, *Treasure Island* (1883).

Mountainous Lochnagar and the waters of the Dee enrich Crathie's vistas while royal associations, its church, the bridge and the lives of early Christian saints distinguish Crathie's history. Crathie borders the Balmoral estate amid Braemar and Ballater.

The villages of Glenmuick, Tullich and Glengairn comprised the parish in the district of Kinchardine O'Neil, which constitutes the current settlement of Ballater. Glenmuick, or *Glean-muic* in Gaelic, describes a narrow valley visited by pigs. It is thought that the area might have been noted for pig breeding. Tullich comes from *tulach* or 'hillock', and reflects the formation of land around the village of Tullich. Glengairn, from *glean-garbh-amhain*, pertains to a hollow or valley containing the water running across the rocky course of the Gairn. Craigendarroch Hill, 'Hill of Oaks', overlooks Ballater. These trees are known to be over 300 years old. An old drove road passes across the B976 just east of Ballater and, skirting Pannanich Wood, leads to Dalmochie and Glenmuick Camp. There was once a community of Newfoundland lumberjacks encamped here while working to provide timber during the Second World War at a time when local forest workers were fighting abroad.

There was a settlement called Cobbletown of Dalmuchie just east of Tullich. It was said that in 1760 the dreams of an old woman brought her to bathe in a bog of that area. Incredibly, this cured her of scrofula, a form of tuberculosis. Colonel Francis Farquaharson of Monaltrie heard of this and built an inn at Cobbletown called Pannanich Lodge to set up a spa there. The lodge and the Pannanich Mineral Wells thereby established the settlement of Ballater.

Sir Patrick Geddes, 1854–1932, was born in Ballater. He was said to be 'the father of town planning' having a deep social concern. He was also a professor of botany in Dundee. His early practice took him to the old town of Edinburgh then to James Court. He improved living conditions in Europe and planned buildings and cities all over the world.

In close proximity to Ballater are the villages of Dinnet, Tarland and Logie Coldstone. Dinnet and the surrounding Muir of Dinnet are overlooked by the hills of Morven and Culblean amid Ballater and Aboyne. Dinnet is deemed by some to be the entrance to the Highlands, while others refer to the pass at Ballater. The village grew from the advent of the railway joining Aberdeen to Ballater in 1866, and its parish was established in 1886. Its first minister was also a notable author called John Grant Michie. Although the rail link ended in 1966, wildlife devotees, historians, geologists and archaeologists continue to visit Dinnet. Accompanying the establishment of Balmoral Castle, Dinnet thrived, its Old Coaching Inn became the Profeits Hotel, which is now called Loch Kinord Hotel, and was established by the nieces of Dr Profeit, who was Queen Victoria's physician when she was in Balmoral. However, the area has a further 5,000 years of history.

The village of Logie Coldstone, another parish in the district of Kincardine O'Neil, was created in 1618 from two very old parishes, unsurprisingly called Logie and Coldstone. The word 'logie' means a low-lying place while the origin of Coldstone or Coldstane is indefinite. Although amid the rivers Don and Dee, the borders are partly delimited by the River Deskry, thus dividing it from Strathdon.

Aboyne was established after 1670. Initially it was named Charleston of Aboyne in recognition of Charles Gordon, first Earl of Aboyne, who partially reconstructed Aboyne Castle (1671) and effectively brought about Aboyne's Charter. Facilitated by Sir Cunliffe Brooks of Glentanar, the advent of a railway from 1853 until 1966 significantly enriched this town, and the nearby village of Lumphanan also grew from the intervention of the railway during the 19th century. However, Lumphanan has an earlier antecedence. Lumphanan was a parish in the district of Kincardine O'Neil, two or three miles north-west of Kincardine O'Neil itself. Lumphanan's church, reconstructed in 1762 and augmented in 1851, was devoted to St Finan prior to the Reformation. The parish precincts encompass a stone that marks the vicinity where Macbeth was killed in 1056 and a motte called the Peel of Lumphanan that had once supported a 13th century fort. Lumphanan was a part of the barony of O'Neil and belonged to the Durward family in the 13th century. It is thought the name Durward derives from the antecedent family occupation of door warden.

Kincardine O'Neil is possibly the oldest village on Deeside, and lies amid Aboyne and Banchory. The holy well of Saint Erchan, who established the village, was sealed in 1858. In 1228 the lands of Onele were presented to Thomas Durward. Durward constructed a bridge here and his son established a hospice for travellers. Other buildings include a 14th century parish church, a tollhouse, an Episcopal Church of 1866, two terraces of 1802 and Kincardine House of 1897. Fairs exhibiting black cattle, sheep and horses were once held in May and September within the village.

Alexander Ross was an 18th century poet from a farming family in Kincardine O'Neil parish. He graduated from Marischal College in 1718 and tutored the children of Sir William Forbes of Craigievar. Ross also taught at Aboyne, Laurencekirk and at a school in Lochlee, Angus, where he ended his days. His poetry was in Scots, encouraged by the poet, James Beattie. Ross published *The Fortunate Shepherdess* in 1768. His work even received acclamation from Robert Burns and was cited by Sir Walter Scott. Alexander Ross was buried at Lochlee where his verses may be found upon other graves.

Banchory was established in 1805 and lies upon the north bank of the Dee, attracting its share of tourism. However, there also continues the practice of various crafts, and the food, wool and timber industry. John Scott Skinner, otherwise known as the 'Strathspey King', was born here in 1843. He was a well known composer of Scottish music and a virtuoso of fiddle playing.

The Kirkton of Durris lies upon the burn of Sheeoch close to its confluence with the Dee, four miles east of Banchory. To the north-east of this village exists a mound upon which the dwelling of previous nobility had stood in the Middle Ages, and to the east is Durris House, which dates to the 17th century. Cosmo Innes (1798–1874), a distinguished antiquary, was a native.

Only five miles from Aberdeen and to the south of the Dee lies Maryculter or the Kirkton of Maryculter, a parish within the lands of Culter (Gaelic: *Cul-tir*, 'the back-lying land'). Devoted to St Mary, the remnants of its kirk are found near Maryculter House, which was originally a chapel of the church at St Peter Culter, now a village named Peterculter. Peterculter arose as a result of the paper mill in 1751. Part of nearby Culter House was built by Sir Alexander Cumin. It is said that the Cherokee Indians made another Alexander Cumin their 'king'. Accompanied by other chiefs of that tribe he symbolically presented his 'crown' in service to George II.

The Knights of St John of Jerusalem administered Maryculter during the Middle Ages, which is reflected in the name of Templar Park nearby. The new church of 1782 contains carved images of Thomas Menzies and his wife, Marion. The Menzies obtained the Maryculter estate in the 14th century. In 1829 John Menzies gave land to a local Catholic diocese to establish Blairs, otherwise St Mary's College.

The journey through the settlements of Donside will start near the hamlet of Corgarff, west of Stathdon. The main church at Strathdon occurs where the Nochty joins the Don and, consequently, that place was originally named Invernochty. This church is sometimes called the Cathedral of the Strath and dates from 1851. Robert Smith writes about a farmer renowned for uncovering a well of remarkably clear water in this parish. Wullie Gray's well was not far from the Tobar Fuar, the 'cold well', said to cure disability, blindness and deafness. It was regarded as being the second largest spring in Scotland and sufficiently powerful to drive a standard-sized mill wheel.

Progressing four miles south-west of Strathdon, where Tornahaish Burn meets with the River Don, we find the village of Tornahaish and a Roman Catholic Chapel dated 1880. Not too far away from here the work of dykers unearthed a cache of silver coins in 1822. They were found on the western side of a hill near Tom Fuaraich, *Tom a' Bhuraich*. The majority of coins were of Henry III's reign, with some from the reign of William I, 'The Lion', and two were of King John's time. There were two rings among the treasure; one was iron gilt mounted with a pale sapphire, the other a gold ring adorned with a much darker sapphire. Coincidentally, in 1829 a similar ring was found in the Bishop of Chichester's coffin, circa 1146.

To the south and east lies the village of Migvie of the Cromar district. The remnants of Migvie Castle, the erstwhile stronghold of the Fraser family, are located here. The churchyard hosts the Migvie Stone, which has a Pictish antecedence from the ninth century. Alternatively, by travelling downstream and looking to the southern bank of the River Don, we reach Towie. Its church of 1803 has an interesting mortsafe, an iron guard placed over a coffin to prevent grave robbing.

Towie and its region were known for producing very good butter. At one time there were located 'butter wells' where it is said butter was cooled on its way to Aberdeen market. Ten miles north of Towie lies Rhynie, the 1600 records of which indicate a farm called Butterbrae that was such a prodigious producer of butter it was able to settle payment of rent in quantities of such dairy currency.

The progression east brings us to Kildrummy and seven miles west of Alford. The kirk at Kildrummy dates from 1805; it presents a remarkable and rare architectural style, being rectilinear with a bow-shaped front. Kildrummy church was sometimes named 'the Chappel of the Lochs' because of the surrounding marshes. The previous church was devoted to Saint Bride, accommodating the burial site of the lineage of Elphinstone.

The village of Alford is amid the Howe of Alford near the River Don, 23 miles west of Aberdeen and south of the Coreen Hills in rich farmland. The Scots word *howe* describes a low stretch of land that must not be confused with the English word of the same spelling, which means a tumulus or barrow.

Alford was a kirkton known for agricultural engineering and its cattle market. A kirkton is a farm town, *fermetoun*, associated with a church and distinguished from the planned villages of recent times. The village grew after becoming a railway terminus in 1859, and then provided residential settlement for people servicing the oil industries of the 1970s. However, the cattle market ceased operation in the 1980s.

Charles Murray was born in Alford on 28th September, 1864. He was initially trained as a civil engineer in Aberdeen, but moved to South Africa in 1888. While abroad he wrote poetry and worked hard to retain connections with his family and homeland. Murray was famous as a champion of the Doric dialect in his writing, and the authenticity of his feeling was keenly expressed. His work was rooted in the life and the land of his birth. A humorous and lively poem called *The Whistle* is a warmly remembered favourite of the people of the region. Charles Murray associates some of his observations to the place names near Bennachie, a 'lowland hill', such an example being the Lord's Throat in the parish of Keig, which related to Lord Forbes of nearby Castles Forbes and the road to that estate. These local qualities were refined in 13 poems in the collection called *Hamewith*, 'homewards', published in 1900, the latter being republished five times while Murray still lived.

After marrying Edith Rogers, Murray had one son and two daughters. He served in the Boer War in 1899 as well as the First World War. Aberdeen University honoured Murray in 1920 with further honours in 1922. Dying in Banchory on 12th April, 1941, Murray's ashes were buried in the churchyard at Alford. Memorial gates exist at Murray Park in Alford and portraits of Murray are kept in Aberdeen Art Gallery, one of which was painted by his daughter, Sheila.

Born in 1912, Elizabeth Forbes-Sempill practiced as a doctor in Alford and was instrumental in securing an important legal precedent and juridical landmark regarding the rights of transsexuals. The Sheriff's Court granted an amendment to a birth certification in 1952 to replace the gender specific name 'Elizabeth' with 'Ewan', upon the latter completing a gender change. Ewan married his erstwhile housekeeper and subsequently inherited the baronetcy of Forbes of Craigievar upon the death of his brother. Although this was challenged, Ewan's entitlement was upheld by the home secretary of the time. Ewan Forbes-Sempill died in 1991.

William McCombie was born in 1805. He was otherwise known as the 'King of Grazers', a famous native of Tillyfour by virtue of the groundbreaking work he accomplished in developing the Aberdeen Angus breed of cattle. A farmer's son, he passed over a university education at Aberdeen to cultivate his father's fields. Becoming a cattle dealer at first and tenant farmer in 1829 he then became a highly successful breeder of cattle. Great respect was afforded his success. He was awarded many prizes, as well as the highest prize at the Paris Exposition of 1878.

A famous specimen of McCombie's endeavours, *Black Prince*, won several awards in 1867. It even came to the notice of Queen Victoria, who enjoyed its beef as a Christmas gift. The Queen even visited McCombie at Tillyfour. He was the first tenant farmer elected to the House of Commons in 1868 and died at home in Tillyfour in 1880. A statue of his work was unveiled there in 2001 by Charles, Prince of Wales, in the presence of Queen Elizabeth, the Queen Mother.

In 1840 Sir Archibald Grant virtually rebuilt the old Kirkton of Monymusk as a village designed for workers and craftsmen of the estate. This included the planting of the renowned Paradise Woods. According to our source, McConnochie, the trees were said to number at least 50 million! In 1170, Gilchrist the Earl of Mar instituted a fellowship of Augustinian canons upon ground reputedly established by Malcolm Canmore in 1078. The Monymusk Stone, of Pictish antecedence, is found at the 12th to 13th century church of St Mary, as well as monuments that mark the lineage of the Grant lairdship. It was an Aberdonian called John Fyfe, 1830–1903, who was responsible for 19th century Kemnay, which grew with the advent of the railway and granite quarries. Kemnay granite was used to build Marischall College in Aberdeen, the Royal Liver Building in Liverpool, the Thames Embankment in London, foundations of the Forth Bridge and the new Scottish Parliament, which was completed in 2004.

An eastward progression will bring us to the royal settlement of Inverurie where the River Don and the River Urie conjoin about 17 miles north-west of Aberdeen. This was the main centre of the Garioch lordship and erstwhile executive centre for the Gordons. The earliest known charter occurs around 1558, but modernity obtained after the establishment of the Aberdonian Canal at Port Elphinstone where the River Don turns, the latter village being the vital link between Inverurie and Aberdeen Harbour in 1806. Travelling south are discovered the remains of the 16th century parish church Kinkell of St Michael, which has a splendid sacrament house dated 1524. Prehistoric stones are also found in this area, not least the East Aqhorthies stone circle and the Brandsbutt sculptured stone.

An indigent handloom weaver of Aberdeen moved to Inverurie at a particular point in his life when he was known for his skill with words. This 'weaver poet', as he was often called, was William Thom. He was the author of *The Blind Boy's Pranks*, *The Mitherless Bairn* and many others.

As we approach the end of this brief excursion through the settlements surrounding the Dee and the Don our course will turn south towards the Dee. On our way, but still Donside, lies the Lyne of Skene; as Smith informs us, its name stems from the Gaelic *loinn* meaning 'meadow' or enclosure.

Another traveller, of the 19th century, came to live out his last years here and has left expressions of that travelling life. We are told that the people of Lyne had impressed him and they in turn had their hearts affected by that expression.

William Chisholm was a poet and an erstwhile heckler or 'flax dresser'. He took to being a packman, in other words a peddler of 'packs' of stationery, travelling even as far as Ireland. Chisholm related his life on the road and sometimes in song. By 1854 Chisholm settled in the Lyne of Skene. The people of Lyne grew very attached to this man, who had little formal education yet was fluent in Byron, Shakespeare and Burns; it was also evident in Chisholm's writing that he was moved and heartened by them. One can only imagine the extent of the stories that Chisholm told and had yet to tell.

The recorded events, lives and landmarks of villages are but some of the examples of characterisation by which places are instilled with a significant present. A sense of place is also derived from its traditional narratives, and this aspect of human association influences the subject of the next chapter.

LONACH HALL – 2000

In eighteen hunner an twenty-three Sir Charles Forbes did hae
A bonfire on the Lonach Hill, for John's majority.
An there an then it wis agreed, a society tae create;
They named it "Lonach" fae that mound, sae history dis relate.

In eighteen hunner and thirty-six, a gaitherin wis held,
For fowk tae meet, an some compete, an tradition be upheld.
In eighteen hunner an forty four, the Lonach men decreed,
They'd big a hall an hae a ball, preceded by a feed.

An there the highlanders wid meet – baith high an low degree;
Tae hae gweed cheer an comradeship, let charity be free.
In eighteen hunner an ninety six, the hall becam ower wee;
A bigger een wi flat wis built, funded by the jamboree.

A sale o work produced some siller, an maistly aa agreed
A hurl in Doctor Howie's car weel worth a tanner a heid.
For mony a year, the hall wis used for fun an fair melee,
For denners, dances, concerts, plays, an mony a weddin spree.

The dance-bands cam fae aa the airts, Hawthorn, Cameron, Shand,
O radio fame, tae name bit three, the best in aa the land.
Bit, time weers on, an eence again, the beild becam ower sma
Tae meet the needs o modern times it wis nae eese avaa.

So, in nineteen hunner an ninety eight, John barber did arrange
For fowk tae meet an hae their say, on fit they'd like tae change.
Noo, aabody there they did agree a new kitchen wis essential.
Said een an aa, the toilets tee, tae be renewed wis vital.

The muckle hall, it wid be kept wi certain alterations;
For new activities tae tak place, an diverse operations.
A steering group wis then convened, wi Sandy Smith in charge;
They made the plans an raised the funds for community at large.

Dee and Don – Inspiration

An so, the Lonach Hall Community Association formed,
A wi, Rob Lowrie in the Chair, the public wis informed.
The firm o "CHAP" it wis contracted tae demolish an rebuild,
They'd cairry oot the transformation that aabody hid willed.

The day they planned his come at last, Phase one his been completed.
The biggin's deen an aathing's clean; it's lichted, plumbed an heated.
On the eighteenth day o eleventh month, Millennium year twa thoosan,
The hale community's gaithered here, tae mark the official re-opening.

The Main Hall his been tarted up, an beastie's heids made clean.
The Forbes tartan's been renewed – by Sir Hamish it wis gien.
So, noo we're here – the stage is set for gran re-opening.
Wi band, a bouncy fort, an teas, wi "Rural" ladies copin.

"The Old Blind Dogs," an separate disco, roons aff the entertainment
We pledge oor thanks tae aa concerned – A toast tae their attainment!

LORNA ALEXANDER

A DEESIDE SUMMER

Dunking our feet
in the River Dee,
catching tiddlers
with bandy nets.

We swan midway,
against the current,
shock in our mouths
breaking heartbeat.

We drank lemonade
on carefree pebbles,
drying like blueberries
sucking rouge.

CATRIONA YULE

Dee and Don – Inspiration

BALLATER BAIRNHOOD

Rage they did till their tongues were sair –
Faith – nettle's a gey short sting,
A skelpit dowp an a grumphin glower,
Ne'er clippit a lintie's wing.

I niver cared, deil nur docken,
They micht grummel, an curse, an bann,
Fur I'd jeloused far the kelpie hides,
Far the peesie wheeps, an the bandie bides,
An the silken birk in the gloaming glides,
An the rabbit roadies gang.

For ilkie teir on a torn frock
Wis a tree I'd shinned alang…
'Twis a stand o velvet trumpeters,
The foxgloves played me a sang.
Them an a choir o bluebells
That keepit me oot sae lang.

An aabody kens that the reidest rasps
Are clasped in the sherpest thorn,
Far the daddylanglegs cried me in –
His wyte that ma claes wis torn.

The pirled hose, an the scrattit legs?
'Twis heather that caad them dane,
'Twis birk an win' on a body's skin
(For aabody kens that a bairn maun climm)
That bladdit ma Sabbath sheen.

I'd try the patience o Job, says you,
Yer wishin I'd niver bin born…
I'll catch ye a salmon – wait an see
The bosker o beezers lowpin the Dee,
Jist dicht the froun far the smile sud be,
I'll be aabody's frien the morn!

SHEENA BLACKHALL

GRANITE'S CHILD

An explosion shatters the quiet heart of Kemnay,
Another slab of granite is won.
It rattles through Donside, the harsh voice of warfare,
Yet soon another infant is born.
The ragged-edged slab is cut, trimmed and squared,
The child in it's cradle protected and warm.

A solid stone block is carved and made font like.
The child's crying voice cuts through smiling Kirk
Whose granite block walls have stood for five lifetimes,
Testament to a former time's works.
No one can measure cold granite's lifespan,
A child soon learns to feel and to talk.

A rough lump of stone waits in the quarry,
The child runs free beneath July sun.
A stone's roughly fashioned by a foresighted sculptor,
The man's life is blessed with a child of his own.
A tablet's raised upright with scribed, polished surface,
The lasting cold record of a life brief but warm.

RICHARD L ANDERSON

THE WAUKRIFE ROGUE

O sleep ma bairnie, ye waukrife rogue, your daddie's far awa frae you and me.
Lie doon an close your sweet blue een, yon same blue een as your faither's be.
He sleeps in trenches, deep wi glaur, in Flanders' field across the sea.
He kens na ye're his bonnie wee lad, I ken na gin he'll live or dee.

He wis the orra loon frae Pitnie's toon, an me, the kitchie deem frae Glenkindie.
He coorted me sae tenderly, wad melt my hert wi yon look at me.
Bit war an strife, tho o'er the Main, gart him respond sae gallantly.
He marched awa wi the Forty-twa, an left the germ o you wi me.

Ye guardian angels tak care that he comes safely hame tae his bairn an me.
Frae gas an bullet, will ye keep him free, an bring him back tae his family.
An o my lad, it's prood he'll be o his wee man wi bricht blue een.
My prayer, I trow, will answered be, an you an me an he'll be three.

LORNA ALEXANDER

Michael Pegler

PINES

ochre giant

the wizened granny

medusa head

the toasted ogre

old grandee

the dour perimeter guard

all birlin in the wind

Brian Lawrie

REFLECTIONS ON THE RIVER DON FROM TOWIE CHURCH

Column of glass – metal – light
air – still, clear – contained water
essence of river – hills – heather
peat – rock – sand – condensed
energy – tenacity – endeavour
peace…..tranquillity…..silence
no sound.

The river Don. Beginning.
hills – clouds – rain – snow – dew.
Sounds – bubbling springs
chuckling over pebbles
whispering under trees
plopping jumping fish
thrashing salmon tails in shallow water
returning upstream to spawn
thunder – deluge
roaring weir
flooding surge round mill-wheel
tumbling turning
machinery – paper mills
hydro electric
ripple of oars
children splashing
young voices
swishing fishing nets
rushing roaring sea.
The end.

Lorna Alexander

THE RIVER DON

Shaded by the trees and bushes the river flows past, finding its way. Whatever is in its way it always finds its destination, the sea.

Every plant touches the water whenever it needs comfort.

The swans are like kings and queens in white ships sailing home.

The ducks are like children playing in the water for the joy of it.

The moles' piles are lighthouses watching the river.

It is the wind that creeps on the stillest parts of the river making it shiver as if an icy hand glides over.

Leaves fall onto the water, finding their own destiny as they drift down the wandering waters.

PETER BANKS

Lonach Gathering, Donside

BILL ANDERSON

Michael Pegler

Ballater

David Gowans

Chapter 8

✢

Tales and legends

The stories that people tell one another will often contain a mixture of faithful report infused with varying degrees of personal elaboration. The blending of such ingredients adds tonality to our picture of individual agency and event. Many tales will also incorporate the vagaries of human perception and sometimes propaganda. However, the symbols adopted as signifiers of meaning in all judgements of truth remain contingent upon an interpretative endeavour.

These accounts provide a trek through the consciousness of people as they engage with symbols, represent their fear and express their desire. Such is the inspiration of the various seasons of their life and times. Tales and legends may entail fiction, but also incorporate the reality of our general human condition.

There are many tales regarding feuds between the families whose estates span Deeside and Donside. One example involves Alexander Gordon, otherwise known as Black Alister, and Arthur Forbes, otherwise known as Black Airter. Alister supported the expulsion of the French in 1560, fought in the Battle of Corrichie in 1562 and was subsequently imprisoned. He became an earnest supporter of Mary Queen of Scots following the clemency she afforded him. He became embroiled in a grim feud between his family and that of the Forbes.

From his castle at Abergeldie, in 1592, Alister succeeded in resisting the plunder of Deeside by the Mackintoshes, known as 'the Great Spulzie'. The invaders moved through the valley butchering Alister's kin, Henry Gordon of Knock. Suspiciously, the Laird of Strathgirnock, Black Airter, was left unharmed. This smelled of treachery to the Gordons, an action worthy of reprisal, therefore, they burned Airter's home while he was away.

Incredibly, peace was restored, albeit temporarily, for more bloodshed was to follow upon the loving liaison that occurred between Francis Gordon of Knock and Black Airter's daughter. Francis Gordon requested a 'thigging', an engagement present, from his prospective father-in-law. For some reason, probably deep-seated resentment, Airter struck him with his sword, thinking it was still sheathed securely, but as the scabbard came loose so did Francis's head!

After this 'mishap' Airter went into hiding while Alister took possession of Airter's estate at Strathgirnock. Airter returned with help and surprised Alister's seven sons while they cut peat on Airter's former land. Airter proceeded to butcher them all. He must have taken great pride in his gruesome task, for he went to the trouble of exhibiting each head impaled upon a spade. When Alister heard the news the shock caused him to fall from the head of the staircase to his death.

Some other accounts posit a history of family names. For example, on the southern slopes of the Craigs of Logie is found the Nine Maidens' Well, where it is said that nine young women were killed by a wild boar, the scourge of the countryside at that time. A young man, a beloved of one of the dead maidens, killed the boar and some say that upon doing so he cried, "For-Bess", Elizabeth being the name of his beloved. Hence the name of Forbes was derived. It is also said that this was the eve of their marriage and the other women were Elizabeth's bridal maids. A stone with the carving of a boar's head was used to mark the spot. Others say this was originally the 'Boar's Stone' where the beast sharpened his tusks. In any case, the Forbes family removed this to their family residence at Putachie in the Howe of Alford, now Castle Forbes, and the head of a boar is subsequently found on the Forbes's coat of arms.

On another occasion it transpired that Malcolm Canmore, King Malcolm III, tamed a strange and massive beast. It is not clear what species classification is appropriate. It might have been anything from a wild boar to a crocodile. Its name, Tad Losgann, literally the 'Toad Frog' does not help, for we know it was a ferocious carnivore. So much food was needed that the king had to tax the people of their cows to feed it.

At the same place lived the widow and son of a poor man called Macleod.

The son grew to be a fine archer, who later married and had a child of his own. When it came time for the poor widow to pay her taxes for the king's beast she was so distraught she sorely wished for someone to kill the animal. The archer took his mother's last cow to where the beast lived on the rocky shores of the Cluny, but the creature was already dead. When the king viewed the scene he assumed the archer to be the cause of its demise.

The archer was to be hung for this offence and his wife ran to him showing deep emotion, as you might expect. The king, although moved by the scene, remained resolute until Alan Durwood intervened and pointed to the pity of losing a fine archer. The king devised a cruel test. MacLeod was to shoot an apple from the head of his child. However, his wife would also be holding his child, while she sat on a horse, upon Tom Ghainmheine. Thus MacLeod was separated from his target by the width of the Dee.

MacLeod took three arrows. Of the spare two, he placed one in his belt and one between his teeth. Repeating, "This is hard!", he strained to bring himself to his task. At last his shot unleashed, 'like a ray of moonlight', split the apple precisely in two. The king asked why three arrows, and the reply received was that should MacLeod miss, or his family be hurt, the archer was prepared to kill the king.

Thinking beyond the initial threat and realising how useful such a man was, the king offered MacLeod service in his guard. MacLeod's refusal contained a barbed explanation. He vowed that given the treatment he had endured he could not love the king enough to ever use his bow in His Majesty's service again. The king in amazement exclaimed, "Hardy thou art and Hardy thou shalt be". MacLeod's heirs were then called Hardy's son or MacHardy.

Strange events surrounded the demise of John Farquharson of Inverey, who was sometimes referred to as Pipan or the Black Colonel. His relatives wanted his burial place to coincide with that of his family at Castletown even though his own wish was to be buried next to Ann Ban, who was Anna Bhuidh Bhan, his beloved. The family's wish prevailing, the Black Colonel's body was interred accordingly.

Incredibly, the next day the body had emerged to lie above the ground. This hideous event repeated itself for two weeks after which time the corpse then extended its jaunts to visit those relatives who were the most stubborn with regard to its burial wishes. The restless spirit of the Black Colonel shook their furniture, manifested strange apparitions and caused terrible noises. Hissing, chilling breath, frightful moans and stares filled their bedchambers at night until they could stand it no longer.

However, attempts to mollify the spirit of the Black Colonel ran into a practical problem regarding the state of the corpse's decomposition and its transportation. Once near the side of the Dee they decided to place the body aboard a boat and tow it towards its preferred destination beside Ann Ban. The rope by which the body was lowered into its grave resisted untying and so was left behind. It was pointed out by his heir, "My father may wish to rise again".

There are accounts of betrayal, revenge and injustice that incorporate rumours of the supernatural. For example, it was said that Caitir Fhrangach, or French Kate, was a powerful witch who could turn into a mouse when it suited her. This made it difficult to catch her. All well and good, but it was also reported that Robert McKeiry was a wizard of even greater skill. Such was his metamorphic prowess that he could become a weasel in order to catch Kate. McKeiry did catch Kate and she was charged with drowning the Laird of Abergeldie. For that crime she was burned at the stake. However, there is more to that tale than merely a suspicion of witchery.

Kate's offence was at the behest of the laird's wife following Kate's revelation of the laird's interest in other women. This remarkable witch was able to invoke a vision of the husband's exploits at sea. These were not entirely nautical operations, for they involved certain attentions paid to another lady. The sight of her husband's infidelity prompted the laird's wife to crave the drowning of the laird, and she begged Kate to bring it about.

French Kate assembled her tools to do the deed. These entailed a large receptacle of water and floating upon it a wooden dish in proxy for the laird's boat. During Kate's chanting, strange events occurred within the tub of water and to the wooden dish. At first a slight trembling, then pulsing vibrations then violent shudders as her spell intensified. The water rippled then lapped then splashed around the dish until it was full and ultimately sank.

Kate told the lady that the laird was now drowned and this claim was later confirmed. At this news the lady's desire for revenge upon her husband turned to grief at his passing. In this change of heart a newly directed revenge emerged and she vented that emotion upon French Kate, who thus was burned to death upon a place subsequently called 'the Rock of Women', Craig-nam-ban near Abergeldie.

Grief and feelings of injustice that sour the soul can turn into a state of general hatred and a thirst for revenge. It is an understandable tendency if loved ones are brutally torn from our care. There was once a very young and happy woman, wife and mother. That is until one day seven of her sons and her husband were hideously butchered during one of the many troubles of their times. Only a small and malformed son, about whom she had previously cared so little, remained to comfort her.

She became an embittered old woman, or carline, and by such anguish she was transformed into the formidable witch of the Glen Gairn. She gnawed and chewed at the mountains, biting her way through the landscape, hell-bent on diverting the course of the River Don through Morven and into the River Dee. In the Glen of Morven along the Weaver's Burn remains proof of her best effort. Luckily this Thunderbolt Carline, Cailleach-Bheathrach, as she became known, found some of these rocks and stones too hard, so she could not complete the job. This channelling was called her den, Sloc na caillich.

An additional haunt of this witch was her cattle enclosure, which can be found on the slopes of Mamie Hill near Glen Finzie Burn. It is also said that the remnants of her house are found upon Morron where deer hinds came to the bewitchment of her voice and gave themselves to her milking.

Other entities besides witches reside in these landscapes. The mythology of the kelpie provides a very strange example. Described as a water horse, a kelpie will lurk in hazardous fords and stalk the deepest pools of rivers. Its gender is always male and it can change shape to appear as a very tall man with dark hair. Its malevolence towards travellers is legendary, for if you are caught by a kelpie you can expect to be drowned, cut into pieces and devoured.

Some tales relate the trapping of kelpies while in their equine form. Bridled in their sleep they are forced to toil for their captors. However, often these bridles are removed by an innocent seeking to feed what appears to be a poor creature. As the kelpie regains his freedom and gallops away he directs his curses accordingly.

The upper reaches of the Don can be crossed at Luib Bridge. It is said there was a time when there was only a wooden bridge at that place. That is before a terrible flood had swept it away. This event held dire implications for one particular man. He was desperate to reach the other side, for his wife was very ill and needed him urgently. A strange figure appeared before him. This very tall man, for that is what he seemed to be, volunteered to carry the husband to the other side. The frantic spouse was sceptical, but he eventually accepted the help proffered. The tall stranger eventually revealed his true self to be that of a kelpie and upon reaching midstream plunged into the water dragging his victim ever deeper. Struggling and kicking the man escaped and managed to find the opposite bank. When the vexed kelpie surfaced he caused the waters to froth with his ire, and propelled a huge boulder at the traumatised escapee. That very boulder was subsequently named the Kelpie's Stone. In time, as other travellers added stones to it, the site became Kelpie's Cairn.

There are further tales about attracting mysterious and undesirable company while travelling in the land. The 'Grey Man' or Am Fear Liathe Mòr is described as a presence accompanying climbers on the summit of Ben Macdhui or in the mountain passes. At other times, the Grey Man is reported as being more substantial, a creature of inordinate height, excessively hairy and hence, very unsettling.

In 1890 a renowned mountain climber called John Norman Collie was making his way to the summit of Ben Macdhui. As he progressed nearer to the summit entirely alone, or so he thought, he heard footsteps behind him. The interval of sound suggested a stride that was three times longer than his legs could manage. The mist prevented Collie from locating the source of the sound, but its persistence and the fear that was instilled in him was enough to motivate his flight back down the mountain. He refused ever to return, convinced that MacDhui was host to a very strange entity.

There are also accounts of goodness and religious narrative. Machar's Well, Tobar Machar, is the setting for such a legend associated with Saint Machar's Chapel at Corriehoul in Corgarff.

There was a time of terrible famine in Corgarff. One day the priest's housekeeper, Martha, expressed her anguish concerning the bareness of her pantry and that of the villagers. The priest went to the well and prayed to

Saint Machar to relieve the suffering. His plea was a solemn one, motivated by unselfish concern. Upon his return he gave the following instructions to Martha. She was told to make a dawn visit to the well. During her visit she was not to look into the well, but walk around it three times in the name of the Holy Trinity before drawing from its depths. However, Martha drew much more than water; three salmon repeatedly filled her pail until the famine had ended.

There is yet another story that incorporates lessons of faith, suffering and miraculous intervention. Nathalan, born at Tullich, was to become an accomplished scholar and a saint. He toiled on the land, tilling, sowing and reaping according to the natural cycle. A terrible famine ensued and Nathalan distributed all his stores to where they were particularly needed, but this left no seed for the next season. Nathalan spread sand across his land as if sowing grain, and miraculously a plentiful crop resulted.

One autumnal morning the people accompanied Nathalan to harvest the crop, but a deluge of driving rain caused the waters of the Gairn and Dee to overflow upon the fields. Everyone including Nathalan doubted the goodness of God at that moment. As abruptly as their faith had deserted them the weather changed. All its destructive force abated and the skies cleared once more.

Clouds of remorse replaced the bad weather. Nathalan's anguish was so intense that he sought penance for his spiritual weakness. He locked a chain to his right ankle and vowed only to remove it upon a successful pilgrimage to Rome. Nathalan emphasised this commitment by throwing the key of his chains into the River Dee. Even now that place is known as the Key Pool.

An arduous pilgrimage followed, Nathalan praying for forgiveness at the numerous shrines of Rome. He eventually needed food, so he bought a fish from a small boy. The very same key that Nathalan had thrown into the Dee at the start of his penance was found within the fish, emerging with no sign of corrosion. As a consequence of the Pope hearing of these events, Nathalan gained ordination as a bishop. During a life of subsequent devotion, and at his own expense, Nathalan built three churches, at Tullich, Coull in Cromar and Bothelin.

The Maiden Stone near Bennachie has various associations. The pinkish granite of which it is made is covered in relief carvings. It is attributed to the

Picts of the eighth century AD at a time when Christianity emerged in the region. The refuge of prayer in the face of evil proves invaluable in a story linked with this stone, and involves the daughter of the Laird of Balquhain. She was baking fresh loaves upon the day of her wedding. While doing this she had a wager with a handsome newcomer. It has been suggested that she was prone to flirtation. The terms of the bet were that her baking would be completed before he could build the road to the summit of Bennachie. If he won then she would agree to become his.

Just as other tales have warned us, one never entirely knows with whom one is conversing when it comes to dealing with strangers, for this outsider was the Devil himself. As you might expect, the Devil did indeed complete his task in supernatural speed, upon which the laird's daughter fled away praying to be turned to stone before the Devil could gain possession of her. That is exactly what happened, for to this day a chunk is missing from the Maiden Stone, where a young maiden slipped through the Devil's grasp just as her prayer was answered.

An account of tales and legends that has incorporated divine miracles, the pursuit of evil presences, equine water spirits, witches, restless corpses and even the Devil must also relate a tale about giants. Given that the previous tale of the Maiden Stone places us in the general neighbourhood, we can relate a story about a gaint who guards Bennachie.

It is said that Jock o' Bennachie had a rival for the love of a lady called Anne. This rival was another giant, Jock o' Noth, from another hilltop called the Tap o' Noth. Upon hearing that the latter suitor had won the affections of Anne, Jock o' Bennachie hurled a huge rock at Jock o' Noth, which travelled towards its target some 12 miles away to the west of Bennachie. Upon seeing it coming, even from that great distance, Jock o' Noth stopped it with his foot. To this day on the hillside of the Tap o' Noth the boulder remains with the marks of Jock o' Noth's enormous feet on one side and Jock o' Bennachie's massive fingers on the other.

It will have been gathered from the preceding accounts how interventions of good, personifications of evil and various forces of human machination seethe within the general traditions of tales and legends. Natural places have also featured significantly in these narratives. Some settings are so full of inherent atmosphere that they possess a legendary status of a different order, one that is more elusive yet rooted in the physicality of the earth itself. The tales that have concluded this chapter will have led us to such a location and will constitute the subject of the next chapter.

MIDMAR STONE CIRCLE
AND BALBLAIR THE OUTLIER

In the haar they seem to shiver,
dance with pleasure in the heat.

They have festivals and rituals:
that certain line-up of the sun
and moon; seasons
of harvest and burning stars.

What are they waiting for,
what have they seen?

Within a wood their god arises,
Phallus, impudent and proud.

From the birse trees to the circle
he will come and stake his claims.

And one by one these maids of stone
will take their silent turn recumbent
underneath the howling skies;

a midwife at their foot and at their head.

GERARD ROCHFORD

THE CORGARF BREW

Residing at the Haugh of Auchernach,
On Noughtyside, a parish of Strathdon,
On this day he has been put to the horn,
Yet another of the men of Corgarff.

For the crime of deforcement, he goes down,
Whilst trying to hide his still in the den.
John Watson, caught by the Sheriff's fine men,
His goods and gear escheat, held by the crown.

But the force goes on without faithful John,
The valleys' needs outweigh the locals fear.
At the town hall jail, John swears he can hear,
The cry and cheer, 'Corgarf Brew — long lives on'.

STEVEN WALLACE

TEN THOUSAND YEARS OF LIFE IN THE GARIOCH

The melt water flows to the sea from hill,
Rushing and flushing all life in its path,
Leaving a meandering wake so still,
A reflection of His power and wrath.
But the grey mass held tight from the ice kill.
Standing so proud above the aftermath,
A beautiful landmark left in the wake,
A beacon to the Mesolithic gate.

Stones face south west, for a view of the sun,
Recumbent flanked by two pillars of stone.
And midsummer rays dance around each one,
This flat slab of rock is the largest known.
Buried in the ring, a story begun,
Of cremated bones in land overgrown.
Orbital clues in locations remote,
Round footprints at the base of the Lord's Throat

From cliff to cliff, the walls of iron sweat
Stood tall. A great testament to the fort,
That stood on the peak in dark silhouette.
Twenty feet around as a last resort
To advancing and to invasive threat,
To fight and rule. A military court.
A stone rampart abuts the outer walls,
The last stone stands until the last man falls.

Dee and Don – Inspiration

With Romanised lower lands in their rule,
The men, on foot and sail, push and pull north.
Days and weeks on gruel, the journey so cruel.
But Agricola fights o'er the Forth,
As tribes learn from the military school,
The cost of freedom and what it is worth.
On the land of Durno, two legions rest,
Five gateways, "stampede": the start of their quest.

But thirty thousand warriors held tight,
On the slopes of the towering hill tap,
To rid their land of the terrible blight,
And to keep their name on the Garioch map.
Calgacus led and bled into the fight
Until joy rampaged on the granite cap.
A deadly peace flowed through the slopes of pine,
In respect of the Mons Grupius shrine.

RICKY THOMAS

WATERFALL

We follow paths but then we wander
beyond the scattering of children;

into the arms of trees, the giving moss,
the darkening growth, the cover of leaves,
trying the anxiety of birds.

There is an ache to trace the source of you.

Hand in hand the messages come through,
you know my feelings, know my thoughts,
my need for you upon this bed of rock.

We overhear the waterfall
filling its depth and always wanting more.

GERARD ROCHFORD

TORNAHAISH JOHN

A remnant from a bygone age,
Trapped in the immortal cage.
Long since his work was done,
Waiting for his day to come.

From Dee to Don, still marching on,
O'er hill and burn, the track is long.
His shrill echoes o'er Cairndoor Hill,
His fighting spirit, is hard to kill.

Once upon a time, he stood tall,
Proudly feared by one and all.
Other routes they had to take,
For they knew he lay in wait.

But not so scared was every man.
The Captain, he made a stand.
The Highwayman fell – laid to rest,
They were free from the fearsome pest.

Not one villager shed a tear,
At last they could live without fear.
At last they could march from Don to Dee,
Safe from danger, the route was free.

But even now, his will lives on,
His last cry still echoes like a song
From the Devil. He still marches on.
The military road belongs to Tornahaish John.

Steven Wallace

Michael Pegler

Deeside Moment I

Di Bumpus

Dawn over Deeside

Patricia Walter

Michael Pegler

Linn of Dee, Inverey

Chapter 9

✦

A Lowland Hill

When a person is said to be charismatic we imply that attraction and influence obtain. Part of that attraction may be aesthetic or physical and part of that influence may be psychological or cultural. Certain dispositions stand out because they seem familiar to us for reasons that are unclear. Even at the very first encounter we feel drawn to their company. They have a stage presence that concentrates imagination and reflects aspiration. Perhaps we sense they have interesting stories to relate. Conceivably we are reminded of some ancient truth regarding our identity or heritage. When such tacit notions affect us, the world gains further significance and its details become personally relevant. Can such impressions similarly accompany the experience of encountering a distinctive landscape?

Situated near the River Don lies Bennachie, which may be considered just a lowland hill, for the altitude of its various peaks do not rise as high as those of most mountains. However, its aspect is certainly mountainous and impressive over an extensive region. Whether we refer to it as hill or mountain I want to say that Bennachie imbues monumental charisma.

A brief look at the geological history of Bennachie sketches a notion of its origins and the birth of its features. Bennachie and its neighbouring ridge south of the Don, Cairn William, essentially constitute an immense circle of red granite. Its rocky tops typify a landscape of tors.

A coarse-grained granite formed at Mither Tap combines red and white feldspars of glassy quartz and black mica. Large red feldspar crystals are embedded in the rock, thereby defining its texture in geological terms as porphyritic. Little Oxen Craig and Little John's Length North embody fine-grained granite with cavities or vugs, which contain smoky quartz.

The granite found on every peak and exposed rock face appears scored by asymmetric marks and fissures. Commonly, this is due to the presence of fine-grained intrusions or aplites, which correspond in appearance to the fine-grained geology at Little Oxen Craig and Little John's Length North. Sometimes coarser fragments are found among the fine-grained intrusions and, uncommonly, a coarse-grained intrusion or pegmatite is clearly visible. At Hermit's Crag are found pegmatites containing smoky quartz of up to four inches long.

Geologists tell us that the inception of these granite formations resulted from violent eruptions of molten magma from deep beneath the ground and its solidification upon the cooling surface some 400 million years ago. Following solidification, a series of changes occurred in certain areas as a consequence of compressive forces, thus causing irregular milky quartz crystals to set in a dark red matrix. These are called quartz breccias and are observable near the path to Mither Tap and the old mill on Rushmill Burn.

The dynamics of glacial history is predominantly a west to east movement of ice that leaves glacial grooves on the rock formations of the summit. After most of the glacial ice retreated a large residue was left in the Howe of Alford. Upon the eventual melting of this glacial residue, a relentless journey that cut deeply into the landscape ensued, and its effect is apparent at My Lord's Throat.

Having briefly noted the dynamics of Bennachie's geological foundations we should now take a journey around extant features, and the rich nomenclature of its topography.

Extending east to west for about five miles, the ridge of Bennachie divides the Rivers Don and Gadie, the latter moving eastwards on the northern aspect known as the 'Back O'Bennachie'. Bennachie's precipitous flanks encircle a level top at around 1,500 feet with several elevations above that height: Oxen Craig at 1733 feet; Mither Tap at 1698 feet; Watch Craig at 1619 feet; Hermit Seat at 1564 feet and Craig Shannoch at approximately 1600 feet.

Mither Tap presents an imposing and timeless profile that dwells on the memory even though Oxen Craig is higher. There are remains of a Pictish Iron Age hill fort on Mither Tap. The Bailies of Bennachie erected a directional indicator there in 1973. The Bailies are a group of people who give their time freely to the aim of preserving and protecting Bennachie.

The east face of Mither Tap is called Craignathunder and the tor to the north is called Nether Maiden. Elevated to around 1400 feet and stretching 600 feet between two crags extends the bed of Jock o' Bennachie or Little John's Length. The latter is associated with tales of the giant guardian whose exploits were mentioned at the end of the previous chapter.

To reach Mither Tap from Pittodrie car park one may go via Stay Know and Hosie's Well at Rushmill Burn to follow the Maiden's Causeway, which also features in the legend of the Maiden Stone mentioned in the previous chapter. Although no longer raised, it still constitutes an authentic route to an ancient hill fort near the summit.

There is a place called Craig Shannoch, 'the hill of foxes', which is reached from the village of Oyne. The path, quite precipitous near the top, entails traversing slanted chunks of granite. Marked by deeply weathered striations, the granite presents a layered aspect. One ancient granite layer projects over a small entrance to Harthill's Cave. It is said that from this cave Laird Harthill observed his castle burning, while hiding there in 1644.

We come to Jock's Sark, a verdant place, where it is said that Jock o' Bennachie dried his shirt near Gill Well, west of Craig Shannoch. Gill Burn runs along a ravine amid Craig Shannoch and Oxen Craig towards Oyne in the north. This burn then becomes known as the Bogie Burn where it joins the Gadie.

Situated in the company of Craig Shannoch and Oxen Craig, Moss Grieve is a modest elevation of rock among heather that is encircled by moss. This area provided arduous living for local peat cutters in the 19th century and was also called Averon Knapp because an abundance of averons or cloudberries grew nearby. We are told that it is still possible for some cloudberries to be found there today.

From Oxen Craig we can see Aberdeen to the east, the Cairngorms to the west and allegedly even the Caithness Hills 80 miles to the north. Clochnaben is observable to the south. The granite at Little Oxen Craig, which stands 1400 feet high, was once quarried for local building purposes. Shannoch Well is found above its treeline and at one time was a place used by those also engaged in peat cutting or shooting. There was a route for hill walkers through 'The Beeches'. The stone and turf table and seats found here were in need of restoration and it is hoped that a weary traveller may now find that aim realised. The path then navigates an arboreal route and passes the limpid water of Gilree Burn, joined by Ryhill Burn as they both enter the Gadie.

Hill Well lies close to Ryhill Burn west of Puttingstone. An erstwhile custom and belief entailed a visit upon the first Sunday of May, which brought good fortune to the first who drank there. In Gilree Burn gully could be found one of several illicit stills during the early 19th century.

Watch Craig, at 1619 feet, is situated 1000 yards west-south-west of Oxen Craig where the three parishes of Oyne, Premnay and Keig coincide. Its best aspect is from the south. One thought is that it could have been an observatory to spot advancing enemies. To the north is Hummel Craig, and half a mile to the north-west is Hermit Seat, at 1564 feet. Moving south-west along the bank, descending progressively to Black Hill, at 1403 feet, the way veers south-south-west to a road adjacent to the Lord's Throat.

A southern aspect reveals the less renowned elevations of Turf Hill and Scarfauld Hill, and the inclines of Shiel-Know and Blackwell Head. At Watch Craig the March Burn begins its travels amid Scarfauld Hill and Blackwell Head to meet the Don approaching Westhaugh.

Eastwards finds Bruntwood Tap and Garbet Tap, beneath which lies quarry hill, previously quarried by an English company in the 19th century to send granite blocks to Sheerness Docks. Ginshie, Garbet and Dalau Burns appear from here and conjoin with Birks Burn. Proceeding west, the burn passes the Mill of Tilliefoure and feeds the Don, also in the region of Westhaugh.

The Clachie Burn journeys south from a low point on the eastern side of an escarpment that divides the main bank from Millstone Hill. Millstone Hill is one and a half miles south-south-west of Mither Tap. Tullymuick is a similar distance north-north-west of Watch Craig. On the top of Tillymuick, 'the Sow's Hill', can be found remnants of an ancient earthwork. These two hills are somewhat separated from the forms of Bennachie.

Bennachie was granted Commonty land (common lands under the auspices of a landlord or number of landlords who allow communal rights of utility, such as peat cutting, grazing livestock or the collecting of building materials) and the first squatter on Bennachie arrived in 1801, building a home next to Clachie Burn in order to manage a very difficult and hard life. This person's daughter married a mason, John Esson. In 1826, John Esson, his wife and son, aged five, returned to build a home in this wild place. From this inception grew a colony of similarly independent and hard working people.

The community that grew had no title to the property they developed, and their associations and conventions were sufficient to their community alone. Given their group was situated on the border of Chapel and Oyne, and because of the responsibilities explicit in the Poor Laws, neither parish came forward to claim them as their citizens. Therefore, 'The Colonists', as they became known, devised their own laws, which also allowed the production of their own duty-free whisky.

As mentioned previously, the Colonists were mostly hard working and responsible people. The Essons were masons and well known dykers in the area. The Macdonalds were retired contractors. Two or three Littlejohn households were thatchers, and Sandy Lindsay was a fish 'cadger' or dealer. The Gardens had the highest situated croft, and the other families included the Christies, Finlaters, Mitchells and Beverleys. Twelve homes constituting 60 people existed there in 1859, but by 1939 only a third generation member of the Esson family, George Esson, remained. The sequence of events that marked this outcome needs an explanation.

The Commonty was partitioned by neighbouring landowners on March 1859 resulting from the juridical process of the Court of Sessions whereby colonists lost squatters rights because the common land had become part of the estate of Fetternear. Initially the rents were small, the mood inclusive and they were even invited to eat all they could at the Grand Rent-Day Dinner. However, five months later greater regulatory impositions had to be assimilated. Consequently, John Essons found himself signing a lease to permit him the right to use his house – the house *he* had built and fields *he* had cultivated from an erstwhile barren environment.

During the 1870s, as profits from crofting reduced and constricted the very life of the colony, its people began to leave. In 1878 John Esson paid two pounds for gardens previously belonging to the Macdonald crofts, and even more evictions took place later that year. The Littlejohns, Hugh and James, either unwilling or unable to pay their rents, desisted from doing so and refused to move. Officers of the sheriff, two policemen and estate workers enforced their eviction. In such impoverished times the population of colonists was reduced to just one. John Esson, being the second on the hill at five years of age, died in 1891 at 70 years of age.

John Esson's youngest son, George, returned from America and lived in the croft for 48 years. George Esson was also a mason and a renowned dyker. He walked great distances to his work and walked back to his croft every night. A great strength of character and independence of spirit was associated with this man. When he died on 31st May, 1939 he was interred in Chapel Churchyard.

There are of course natural histories to be considered when assembling a conception of a place. In woodland areas we find juniper and blaeberry. There are two separate sites where it is possible to find the orchid, *goodyera repens*, and rare *linnaea borealis*, after the Swedish naturalist Carl Linnaeus. Only an inch or two high, the latter has two pink bell-like flowers from a single stem attributing to it the common name of twinflower.

Scotts pine and Sitka spruces occur on Scare Hill and Millstone Hill. Dense plantations of spruce and Douglas fir allow only mosses and fungi to thrive. When not too crowded they enable heather. Where deciduous larches grow, wood anemone, chickweed wintergreen and wood sorrel can also survive.

These examples of symbiotic relations between living organisms underwrite the need for careful management to retain biodiversity. The term 'climax vegetation' refers to plant life that would naturally be left extant in an area if the environmental conditions of that site were stabilised by being left undisturbed for an extended duration. The term denotes the ultimate plant ecology that would remain forever under those conditions unless destabilised by further intervention or event. Scots pine is part of the climax vegetation for this place, which means that if heather moor is left alone there is a natural progression to birch and then pine, where heather can also continue. However, spruce does not provide a progression that necessarily includes heather, so growing spruce is not natural in that sense of appropriate climax vegetation, and it is hard to grow spruce among heather.

There are notably two birch species in the area. The smaller birch, *betula pubescens*, is more common to Bennachie and the taller, *betula pendula*, is more common to Deeside. Generally, there is far less oak, however, there are oak woods above the Place of Tilliefour on Millstone Hill. Woodlands also host various fungi such as fly agaric and elf cups.

The animals that populate the area include fox, stoat, weasel, pheasant, rabbit, hare, roe deer, occasional red deer and red squirrel. Bird populations include blackcock (male black grouse), wood pigeon, wood cock, thrushes, blackbird, four species of tit, golden crested wren, cuckoo, warblers, sparrow hawk, greater spotted woodpecker, treecreeper, finches, buntings, magpie, crows, jay and the rare capercaillie, the world's largest grouse. Other rare bird species recorded are the great grey shrike, crossbills and even the hoopoe.

The moorland habitat is mostly ling heather, and in the middle of August the hill is transformed to a rich purple. Other heath species do occur there. In the wettest areas exist cross-leaved heath, *ericaceae tetralix*, with pale pink, occasionally white, flowers. Drier areas sustain a close relative, *ericaceae cinera*, or bell heather. This heather enriches the hill in July with a deep red colour. The latter is important for producing the dark honey of the area. Bearberry, *arctostaphylos*, is found in soil on granite substrate adjoining the Mither Tap path beyond Heather Bridge. Where there is more peat, at higher elevations we may find crowberry among blaeberry. Blaeberry, *vaccinium myrtillus*, is a deciduous plant while the cowberry, *vaccinium vitus-idaea*, is evergreen. The latter, also called cranberry, is often used in cooking sauces and jellies. As mentioned elsewhere, averons or cloudberry, *rubus chamaemorus*, are also found on this moorland.

Where the peat is wet there exist species of cotton sedge. The tufted heads of these plants might have filled pillowcases in earlier times. The sphagnum mosses also occur here. In the past they have served to dress injuries, for they can soak up blood and, to a limited degree, cleanse and protect a wound from further infection. The insectivorous sundew, *drosera*, and butterwort, *pinguicula*, are both found near Rushmill Burn. Where the heather is shorter on the summits, clubmosses are present. The latter are often present in regions of the tundra and are relatives of ferns. Bennachie hosts alpine clubmoss, *lycopodium alpinum*, and fir clubmoss, *lycopodium selago*, while at lower elevations common clubmoss, *lycopodium clavatum*, and jointed clubmoss, *lycopodium annotinum*, are sustainable.

The fauna supported by this moorland might include the blue mountain hare, rabbit, shrew, mouse, vole, grouse blackcock, ptarmigan, meadow pipit, snipe, curlew, golden plover, hen harrier, kestrel, short-eared owl, buzzard, lizard, slow-worms and adders. The sighting of a ptarmigan or adder is rare.

Apart from Bennachie's influence in other chapters of this book, the brief notations that have been possible in this space have attended to the dynamics of Bennachie's birth in geological time, and the characteristics of the substrata as it emerges at its peaks. Along the way a wealth of history-laden nomenclature has been considered. Human events have been set within topographical detail, and the biodiversity that animates the various features of Bennachie's slopes has been visited accordingly.

This short excursion has confirmed in my mind that which was broached at the start of this account. There is an indefinable potency in the land of Bennachie, first impacting upon your senses and then upon your intellect. I want to say that by analysing its parts we can explain its character, but that falls short of conveying its full value. I want to say that we can account for its atmosphere by noting its history, but that falls short of conveying the many layers of interest it personifies.

As we contemplate, standing upon Mither Tap or Oxen Craig, we can appreciate the prospect Bennachie has provided, both in actuality and conceptually. We may simply conclude that the perspective it affords is extensive in its influence; here we are indeed well placed to regard many paths of enquiry, including the imminent theme that focuses our gaze towards the city of Aberdeen and the estuaries of these two rivers.

PORTRAIT OF A FORT

From cliff to cliff, the walls of Iron sweat
Stood tall – a great testament to the forte,
Twenty feet around, as a last resort
From those of Durno – an invasive threat.
On the top, the Tap ran constantly wet,
While the camp below awaited support
To fight and rule. A military court
That watched the peak as a dark silhouette.
But now the walls are hidden, torn apart
By fifteen hundred years of feet on rock
And wind and rain – a waterfall of block
That distracts as one enters the rampart.
We are told, what goes up must then come down,
Refuge walls cascading, now a ghost town.

RICKY THOMAS

THE NATIVE

So I came back to the North-east
Back to where I yearned to be
Found my burn and my river
And my mountain – Bennachie

Heard the song of the Gadie and Don
I'd kept in my heart through the years
Walked the remembered pathies
Up the "blue hill", mist or clear

"Come awa, wee wifie"
My Grand-dad used to say
Leading and carrying me up the hill
When I was jist a bairn

"Come awa, wee wifie"
I hear my brothers call
As we skipped to the top in all weathers
With hardly a rest at all

"Come awa, wee wifie"
They're crying to me still
But now they need to take my arm
To help me up the hill

With the last "Come awa, wee wifie"
It'll aye be my home
So take up my casket and scatter my dust
When my climbing days are done

GRISELDA SARAH MCGREGOR

Sunset over Bennachie

RAY LIVERSIDGE

Michael Pegler

'Bennachie'

Norman Thomson

Chapter 10

The journey ends

Fresh current merges with brackish water in the estuarial margins of the Dee and Don. Their courses through Scotland's third largest city runs closer than at any other stage of their journey and their ending is variously realised in a modern harbour and the sandy coastline of the North Sea.

Dating from the seventh or eighth centuries, Aberdeen is alternatively named 'the Granite City' and the 'Flower of Scotland', being well known for its parks and gardens. The three castles displayed on Aberdeen's coat of arms symbolise strongholds previously situated on the three hills of Aberdeen; St Catherine's Hill, Castle Hill and the Port or Windmill Hill (Gallowgate). King Robert the Bruce defeated the English army near Aberdeen and it is said the password used to start the Scots' advance became the city's motto, 'Bon Accord'.

Human intervention has configured the Dee estuary into a significant harbour. The Aberdeen Harbour Board administers, maintains and improves 350 acres of land and water, four miles of quays and 20 deep-water berths. The latter accommodates the handling of five million tonnes of cargo every year. There are three distinct areas in the harbour apart from its dry dock. The first area entails three docks to the north of the estuary; Victoria Dock, Telford Dock and Albert Dock. The second area consists of the Navigation Channel and River Dee Dock on the south bank. The North Pier, the South Breakwater and the Inner South Breakwater reclaim the third area from the sea.

The North Pier was developed during the 18th and 19th centuries. The estuary's tendency to silting once limited access to vessels with shallow hulls. Larger ships had to wait in the deeper areas of the river channel.

A new channel was created between 1869 and 1873, which facilitated the reclamation of an improved harbour.

A picture of the Dee estuary from previous centuries would reveal a narrow channel blocked by banks of sand and an enormous rock called the 'Knock Metellan'. This was cleverly removed by David Anderson of Finzeauch, and contributed to his nickname 'Davie do a thing'. Davie attached the Knock Metellan to a ring of empty barrels, the buoyancy of which set the great boulder adrift so that it could then be towed away.

Salmon constituted the first tradable commodity, but by the 12th century, cloth, wool and hides were also being exported to Flanders. Commerce was established with the Baltic in the 15th century and close links were forged with Danzig. In 1665, Sir Patrick Drummond, 'Conservator of Scottish Privileges', notes that the revenues Aberdeen attracted surpassed all other Scottish towns. Trade was indeed global; maize from Constanza on the Black Sea, timber from Scandinavia, fertilisers from South America, and freight services from West European ports and Canada.

At the north bank of the Dee estuary there is an old fishing village, Footdee, consisting of two groups of cottages. The older name is Fittie or Futty. First noted in 1398, its origins are probably medieval or even older. From Footdee was produced the Aberdeen Clipper, a type of fast sailing ship. The concavity of their bows and the backward rake of their masts added to their speed.

The 1850s witnessed the ships *Stornoway* and *Crysolite* lead a swift trade with the Chinese tea markets. After 1852, many other clippers were being made to set course for China. There was also cargo and passenger business from Australia and South Africa. The 1860s saw other great ships such as the *Flying Spur*, *Yangtse*, *Black Prince* and *Jerusalem*. The *Thermopylae* of Aberdeen was the fastest in the world, even surpassing the *Cutty Sark*, out of the Clyde.

Renowned companies such as Alexander Hall, Walter Hood, Hall Russell and Duthie launched 3,000 ships over two centuries. The Hall yard operated from 1790 to 1957 creating some of the finest sailing vessels and the first clipper ship, the *Scottish Maid*, in 1839. From the 1890s, Hall's built hundreds of steel steam trawlers. Hood's also built some of the world's fastest sailing ships, over 100 ships between 1839 and 1881, including the *Thermopylae*, *Centurion* and *Wooloomooloo*.

Dee and Don – Inspiration

Hall Russell began in 1864 making cargo steamships, later launching fleets of fishing vessels, warships and passenger ships. The last ship built in Aberdeen, the *St Helena*, was launched on the 31st October, 1989. The closure of this shipyard, shipbuilding in Aberdeen, was in 1992.

The late 12th century saw the lands of Torry in the hands of the Abbot of Arbroath Abbey. The growth of Torry entailed two villages, Upper and Nether Torry. The latter was the forerunner of Old Torry, a fishing village realised in the late 18th and early 19th centuries. Most of this village was removed when the Dee was diverted in 1871 and in the 1970s during the harbour's expansion. Currently, only a few houses remain, and none pre-date the 19th century. Sea oil and gas were found in the 1960s and by 1973 Shell UK signed an agreement with the Harbour Board to develop Old Torry village at Maitlands Quay. Similar contracts ensued with other oil companies and subsequent oil production started in June 1975.

Robert Stevenson, the grandfather of the literary author Robert Louis Stevenson, designed Girdleness Lighthouse on Girdleness Peninsula. Its operations ceased around the late 1980s. Girdleness was first lit in 1833 and even today it functions as a navigation marker. Its famous foghorn is called the 'Torry Coo'.

Eighteenth century Marischal Street was possibly the first thoroughfare designed for Aberdeen. Starting from Regent's Quay, at the harbour, it runs uphill to the centre of Aberdeen and Castle Street.

Three distinct municipalities constituted Aberdeen. Old Aberdeen was founded on its university and cathedral, close to the Don estuary. Woodside was a mill town upstream from the Don estuary. 'New' Aberdeen contained a trading community and fishing industry. Aberdeen's centre dates from the 12th–13th centuries, at which time the main focus was a street next to the harbour called Shiprow. The simple dwellings of fishermen and waterfront traders would have congregated along the inlet of Den Burn at its confluence with the Dee estuary to constitute a rudimentary harbour.

The approach to Aberdeen across King VI Bridge or the Bridge of Dee via Holborn Street will lead to the western end of Union Street. Aligned east to west, the latter is a significant thoroughfare, one mile long and over 68 feet wide. The eastern end of Union Street starts at Castle Street, originally Castlegate. The latter was initially Castle-*gait* or *the way* to the castle.

In 1264 Richard Cementarius, Aberdeen's first provost, repaired the Castle (of Castlegate), which dates from 1249.

In 1796, the surveyor, Charles Abercrombie, proposed a new street for Aberdeen to access the land west of the town. The latter thoroughfare would occur west of Castlegates, across a truncated St Catherine's Hill and over Den Burn by incorporating a bridge and a viaduct. Designed by Thomas Fletcher, it crosses the Den Burn in a single span. Begun in 1800, the latter was given the name Union Street in recognition of the Parliamentary Union of Great Britain and Ireland.

The building of Aberdeen incorporated a lot of granite. The first granite quarry, initiated in 1604, produced sills and lintels. Two other quarries were started in 1730 and 1740. Until the end of 18th century large scale projects were not forthcoming. At Rubislaw quarry, granite was extracted for 200 years creating a hole 400 feet deep, 800 feet long and 700 feet wide.

Provost Ross's House is on Shiprow. It is reputedly the second oldest domestic dwelling in 'New' Aberdeen. It was built in 1593 along with its adjoining houses, one of which is now the Maritime Museum of Aberdeen. The Provost Skene's House is located near St. Nicholas House, a multi-storey building of the 1960s. The former is of the 17th century, but its deeds start in 1545. According to the latter criterion, it is older than Provost Ross's House. The successful trader, Sir George Skene of Rubislaw, bought the house in 1669 extending it with new wings and towers, as well as an ornate doorway.

George Keith, Fifth Earl of Mar, founded Marischal College in 1593. Its neo-gothic façade is at the eastern end of Broad Street. The college was first convened in the old building of Greyfriars Monastery as a specifically Protestant university for Aberdeen. The new building was designed by Marshall MacKensie and opened by King Edward VII in 1906. At the time of its opening it was the second largest granite building in the world.

The ancient churchyard of St Nicholas (c.1157) has undergone some recent alterations to its interior, which have unearthed some interesting archaeological findings, not to mention countless skeletons, which would suggest the site has a much longer history than records provide. Measuring 255 feet, it was the largest parochial church in Scotland with a carillon of 48 bells. Its interior was divided into separate places of worship following the Reformation, and its exterior encompasses a charming churchyard.

Leaving Castlegates, on the right, is St Andrew's Episcopal Cathedral, designed by Archibald Simpson in 1816. It contains the Seabury Memorial restoration by Sir Ninian Comper. The latter is a gift from the Bishops of the American Episcopal Church marking the event of Samual Seabury's ordination in Aberdeen, in 1748, as the first Episcopal Bishop of the United States.

Old Aberdeen may be reached via Broad Street, Gallowgate, Mounthooly, Kings Crescent, Spital and the College Bounds or via Kings Street, which was opened in 1800. After Kings Street, one turns right on to Merkland Road, which passes Pittodrie Park, the football club. St Machar Drive is soon discovered turning left into Old Aberdeen. The Town House is to its south, and its eastern end faces the High Street. North of St Machar Drive, the Chanonry leads to St Machar's Cathedral. The oldest inhabited domicile in Aberdeen is the Chaplain's Court, No 20, The Chanonry. The latter was part of an extensive development by Gavin Dunbar in 1519, housing 20 vicars or chaplains.

King David 1 of Scotland transferred the Holy See from Mortlach (Dufftown) to Old Aberdeen. The latter was then a village called the Kirkton of Seaton. Old Aberdeen, variously named Aulton (Old Town) or Seaton (Sea Town), staddles both sides of the Buchan Road. This was a place of considerable importance even at the end of the ninth century.

Situated where the river's course resembles the form of a shepherd's crook, St. Machar's Cathedral has a substantial aspect. There are heavy buttresses, machicolated towers and battlements along its parapets. A magnificent window, of an entirely unique design, fills its prominent twin towers. It is thought the window was the work of a local stonemason.

Machar was a companion of St Columba of Iona. According to legend, Machar dedicated a place of worship on this site as early as AD 580. Bishop Matthew Kyninmond established the first cathedral, but it was pulled down by Bishop Cheyne. The original Norman building doesn't survive except for a single stone that is preserved in the carterhouse above the porch. The new cathedral was commenced in 1357, but the initial plans were not completely achieved. The creation of the cathedral involved several bishops. The following list notes the duration of their office in parenthesis.

Bishop Kyninmond (1135–1138) was responsible for the west towers and he also began work on the nave. Bishop Elphinstone (1483–1513) established a central tower and the south transept. Unfortunely the structure of the central tower failed in 1688. Bishop Elphinstone was also the founder of the University of Aberdeen and a Chancellor of Scotland. Bishop Gavin Dunbar (1518–1532) was another Chancellor of Scotland and he facilitated the cathedral's twin spires and the building of it heraldic ceiling, dated 1520.

In the early years of Malcom IV's reign there was a seminary in Old Aberdeen. Bishop Elphinstone sought permission to establish a university from James IV and Pope Alexander VI. In 1494 a university was granted and dedicated to St Mary under the patronage of the king. The subsequent King's College is situated south of St Machar's Cathedral. The former is surmounted by an impressive architectural structure, styled in the form of an imperial crown. There is also the College Chapel, to the east of the college bounds, built in the 16th century. In 1860 King's College was linked to Marischal College and eventually became the University of Aberdeen. King's College concerned itself with the arts and divinity, and Mariscal College concentrated on medicine and law.

North-west of the cathedral is Seaton Park containing the foundational mound of an ancient timber fortress, the Motte of Tillydrone. Nearby stands a renovated building called Benholm's Lodgings. Adorned by the sculpted image of a knight, the building is commonly referred to as the Wallace Tower. It is constructed according to a 'Z-plan' and was first situated in the middle of Aberdeen. It was relocated in 1963, after which its first tenant was Dr W Douglas Simpson, Scotland's leading expert in medieval castles.

The district of Tillydrone, and other villages in the area, housed the workforce of industry along the lower reaches of the Don. Downstream we come across the Gothic arch of the ancient Brig o' Balgownie (described in chapter four) just a few hundred feet west of the Bridge of Don. Between these bridges lies the small island of Allochy, the site of the Don Mills, and a distillery was established there in 1798.

The river was navigable up to the Don Mills until 1831. Woodside was a group of villages north of the river, incorporating Tanfield, Cotton, Middlefield and Old Cruives. The area called the Printfields was derived from the calico printing works. The works at Tanfield was granted a lease that warranted three workers' lives, whereby should a life be lost one had to be replaced according to the wishes of the taxman and upon the payment of 25 pounds duty, or fine, every year. Although there was not a tradition of a tannery at Tanfield, it may have been that some residual association to the trade existed in that area. Cotton was so named because of its association with Gordon of Cottoune in 1625.

The estate of Woodside was on 'Smithy-haugh', or 'Smith-field'. Cruives is variously called 'Old Cruives' and 'Crofts' in the Abderdeen Charter of 1440. It was also called 'Crwuys' under James III's Charter of 1465. The name is generally linked with the practice of harvesting salmon in traps. A cruive is a type of trap, a kind of dam, often set into a weir. It is stated in 1664 that cruives were built and renewed near the mouth of Scatter Burn or Cruive Burn; however, the Earl of Mar proceeded to destroy them. Other cruives were set opposite Gordon Mills.

Woodside hosted other industries after fishing, including Waulk Mills, Snuff Mills, Bleachfields, Calico and Cotton Mills. The general site was called the Woodside Works.

'Waulk Mill' and 'Waulking' may need a brief explanation. As the name suggests, the cloth was at one time walked upon or rolled with a log or pole dragged behind horses. About 150 – 200 years ago, workers, particularly women, may have attended a long table and kneaded wet, conditioned fabric. Usually 'conditioning' included a soaking in hot urine.

The firm Gordon, Barron and Co. started a printfield in 1785, which produced linen and cotton goods and employed approximately 1,000 workmen. Work 'lads' were accommodated in the 'barracks' west of the works. This was only the second cotton mill to be introduced to Scotland and they closed 80 years later. The Woodside Works was without tenants until the arrival of a paper manufacturer, Alexander Pirie and Sons Ltd.

South-east of Cruives Dykes are Gordon's Mills and the upper premises were occupied by Alexander Hadden and Sons, of the woollen and carpet industry. Paper was made here in 1696 and cloth manufacture obtained in 1703.

Makers of linen thread and cloth, the firm of Granholm began in 1749 at Gordon's Mills. In 1792 the operation of a bleach field was agreed and then a mill lade was constructed. A lade is an artificial watercourse that drives a mill. This one was over one mile long starting from Downie Hill and rejoined the Don below Cruive Dykes. Construction of this lade entailed cutting through solid rock.

In 1805 the extraction of large quantities of water generated a contest of water rights in the courts that lasted 20 years. The industry ceased for awhile in 1848, but restarted in 1859 following the establishment of another company, J & J Crombie Limited of Cothal Mills, who transferred their business to the Granholm works until their closure in the 1990s.

The Granholm Lade is channelled through Persley Den. This is a tree-lined gorge between the Brig o' Balgownie and Persley Bridge. When Old Aberdeen was united with 'New' Aberdeen it contributed the resources of the Commonty of Perwinnes and Scotstown Moor. Perwinnes Moss covered 229 acres at the time and yielded peat and fuel for Old Aberdeen and Corsehill.

The Don enters the estuary at approximately 75 yards east of the Bridge of Don. At one time this estuary may have entered the sea in the Dee harbour. Ptolemy noted the Dee and the Ythan, but said nothing about the Don, perhaps thinking it to be a tributary of the Dee. We are sure that over the years the position of the Don's mouth has varied. The maps by Gordon of Straloch in 1650 indicate the Don turning south to Broad Hill. Shifting sands and floods were probably conducive to such changes.

To ameliorate the negative effects on fishing, Professor James Gregory MD of Kings College built a dyke by 1st June, 1727. It was 430 yards long and was constructed to keep the Don flowing eastwards. During its construction workmen found a previous dyke. A further 262 yards of dyke, seawards, augmented 'Gregory's Bulwark', at a later date. At one time commercial fishing occurred as far as 2640 yards up the Don. Sea fishing operated between the boundary stones on Broad Hill and Berry Hill. Stake nets were erected in 1822 north of the Don and until 1727 small vessels sailed close by the river channel.

Just two miles of sand separates the estuaries of the Dee and Don at the coast. Groups of bottlenose dolphins may be seen in the entrance to the port's navigation channel, and smaller harbour porpoises are visible from the beach. Salmon pass through Aberdeen harbour every spring and diverse species of bird life obtain, such as cormorant, the visiting golden eye and the red-breasted merganser. Along the shoreline fine sand swirls amid feeding birds. Their elegant bills dip to a constant tempo while multiple legs strut in a single congregation.

Standing on Torry Point we see a vessel approaching harbour; battling with the swell it makes very slow progress. We gaze at the undulations of the North Sea and reflect upon previous waters, at the start of our journey, rising among mountains of granite and rolling moorland. The line of the small boat's deck tilts at impossible angles; it falls from foaming white peaks and negotiates its course through deep serpentine valleys. We realise a journey has been completed.

JUST TO HEAR YOUR VOICE AGAIN

River Dee, Garthdee

Down the steep bank
where foxgloves
dip heavy
like salmon rods
across the water,
past the elegant
beech, standing with
such sisterly assurance,
through the little
meadow of stitchwort
showing their cheeky faces
among the bluebells
and campion,
to stand by
the willows (who love
these watery margins
like I do)

just to hear your
voice again.

BRIAN LAWRIE

ESTUARY

Beyond the rabble of invasive fern,
where sky lays hands upon the earth,
a river pauses for final benediction.

In infancy
this river burst through the rock,
grew to uproot boulders, tear out trees,
seduce salmon, promise gold,
nurture and murder cattle.

Now it seems peaceful,
spending a day by the sea.

But the river is loosing its grip,
holding on to shifty banks
and seeped with sand;
its tongue anointed with salt.

River is drowning,
forever drowning,
river, river is drowning.

GERARD ROCHFORD

BRIG O BALGOWNIE (1)

Brig o Balgownie, stoot's thy waa,
Lang shaddas o heich trees doonfaa,
Onno the wrunkled watter's broo,
Roon banks lulled bi the Don's balloo.
Abeen its archwye, cauld an black,
It cairries cobbles on its back,
Far traivellers dauchle, watchin dyeuks
In convoy, sail fur shady neuks.
Snaadrifts o clouds slide saft thegither
In archetypal simmer weather
Far Don tynes its identity
In the braid quicksans o the sea.

SHEENA BLACKHALL

BRIG O BALGOWNIE (2)

Sheela-na-gig: Celtic female fertility symbol

The arch, reflected, shows Sheela-na-gig
Flauntin her braid fertility, as if tae prig
Mankind tae breech the portals o the brig.
Blue kingfisher flees faist, his name tae bigg,
While dugs stravaig tae sniff an pee unchyned
Mangst reeds that doos micht chuse their reefs tae thigg.
The God o watter looed this bonnie rig,
Fin he howked oot a bed tae haud the Don,
Flanked bi the shady willow's dreepin twig
Ower yon Veenetian gondola, the swan.

SHEENA BLACKHALL

DEE FROST

Sharp, clear, cold.
All around,
Sparkling, glistening,
Glinting in the sun,
Frost is everywhere.
From the lower branches of
The Alder, Ash and Sycamore
Along the riverside
Hang icicles,
Stiff, unyielding, immobile,
Linking land and water
In uncustomary union.
Ice to ice,
White on white
Solid, rigid, static
But dignified
And beautiful –
Winter.

Isobel N Archibald

TWIXT DEE AND DON

As I haud ower the Slack these days,
My hert loups in my briest.
"I'm hame," it saft, bit clearly says.
As Deeside faulds me in its airms again.

I'm muckle torn 'tween these valleys twa;
Ane o Don, faar aince I bade;
A couthy land, the fowk are grand,
Bit Dee is aye my hame.

The Parks laid oot aboot my feet,
The rows an peaks o hills;
Far Lochnagar stauns ower it aa,
Glowerin files fan coorse wins blaw,
Or glintin in the simmer sun.
It's aye a sign o granite strength
For aa us mortal fowk.

Beery me deep in Deeside grun,
For there my life began;
An many thochts o days lang syne
Bring furth the ghosts o them I kent
Amun the hills o hame.

Wanderin by the silver stream
I throw the shackles aff o cares an' woes,
(For faa his nane?)
An I'm like a bairn again.

The hills an glens are here for me,
Tae rest an think an be mysel.
My sowl, clean, refreshed aince mair
Is quaet an calm – "I'm hame!"

MARY MUNRO

ICE DANCE ON THE DEE

Each day the river scene is different – at times it is lively and noisy, the water tumbling and rushing over the stony bed with mallards quacking incessantly in competition with raucous cawing from the rooks in the adjacent field but today's scene was something else. Stillness and quietness in the atmosphere, hard frost in the air. Underfoot the river path was solid, packed with ice and snow, so one didn't choose to linger in the near Arctic conditions but one had to stop momentarily to take in the quiet beauty.

There were ice floes moving gracefully down-stream, one after the other, steadily and silently but for a relentless whoosh. The effect was almost mesmeric. Fascinating to watch the non-stop stream of slow moving ice, each shape and size so different. On and on. The river surface was broken up, white and hoary, progressing slowly like a giant jigsaw on the move.
There was an eerie quality in its endless procession.

Further down river the floes were suddenly sucked into turbulent currents. Here they were broken up as if in the jaws of a grinder. They emerged split and crushed and were swept along in a frenzied swirl, fractions of their former glory nearing their journey's end.

Isobel N Archibald

SWANS ON THE LOWER DEE

The swans and their cygnets swim below the derelict decking of the Shaakin' Briggie south of Cults. Now a peaceful backwater, the river here is home to birds, fish and the ghosts of times past. Summer salmon, darting silver beneath the surface, pass the swans on their tenacious way home to the higher reaches of the Dee. The swans stretch their necks, eyes scanning the spectral shadow of an older bridge, an earlier century. From north to south, ring faint echoes of feet crossing its swaying footway, men dressed in sober black, women in their bonnets and Sunday best – all following the call of the bells from Banchory Devenick Church.

Eastwards the little family glide now, under the old Bridge of Dee, whose ribbed arches ring with the clash of a three-hundred-and-fifty year old battle between Royalists and Covenanters. They leave the seventeenth century behind and travel on below the summer-sparkled granite of the King George the Sixth Bridge, busy with morning traffic.

They pause to feed near the Duthie Park, where the river darkens and deepens. Above their heads the Railway Bridge resounds with the rumble and clatter of trains travelling south. Swimming more slowly, they approach the graceful span of the Suspension Bridge, knowing that soon they must turn and go back – for they are not far from the harbour now. Faint smells of ships, sea and fish houses hang in the air. On their right, the glowering bulk of Craiginches Prison rises above them, casting a grim shadow over their perfect white beauty.

Ahead of them, the bustle of Victoria Bridge sounds a warning to go no further. The water flows thicker here, scummed with debris, oily with the trail of ships and dangerous to the swans and cygnets with the salt swell of the sea. Seagulls scream and taunt them with raucous cries, jealous of territory they have made their own.

The family day trip over, the swans turn and begin their homeward journey towards the calmer waters below the Shaakin' Briggie.

MOIRA BROWN

SONG OF THE MORN

The early morning glow
River rushing, roaring by
On the far bank dippers nest
Back and forth, they busily fly.

Gentle primroses so bright
Cheerful birdsong in the trees
Jewelled cobwebs brush my face
As tightropes slung atween leaves

The young green growth, the catkins too
Grey pussywillow by the water
Sight and sound and smell –
Spring has come to the Don

The air is cold, the sky is blue
The sea shines like a golden mirror
All around the light
Brings the Midas touch to the trees.

GRACE BANKS

From the Bridge: Summer

Clare McCarthy

Michael Pegler

Autumn Cogs

Ricky Thomas

Paper Mill 1

Rosemary Taylor

Michael Pegler

Fire Tree

Clare McCarthy

Michael Pegler

Bibliography

Aberdeen City Council, 2006,
Aberdeen's Maritime Trail – A guide to Aberdeen's Maritime Connections,
(Aberdeen City Council), [Museum Pamphlet].

Fraser, G. M., 1921, *The Old Deeside Road – Its Course, History, and Associations*,
(Aberdeen: Aberdeen University Press).

Graham, C., 1984, *Portrait of Aberdeen and Deeside*, 3rd edn,
(London: Robert Hayle).

Grant, J., [1876], *Legends of the Braes O' Mar*, (Aberdeen: Lewis Smith & Son).

Jamieson, D., and Wilson, W. S., 2003, *Old Lower Deeside*,
(Glasgow: Stenlake Publishing).

Marshall, R. K., 2003, *Scottish Queens – 1034–1714*,
(East Lothian, Scotland: Tuckwell Press).

McConnochie, A. I., 1985, *Donside – Aberdeenshire Classics*, 12nd edn,
(Aberdeen: Bisset).

Munro, D. & Gittings, B., 2006, *Royal Scottish Geographical Society,
Scotland – An Encyclopaedia of Places & Landscape*, (Glasgow: Collins).

Murray, I., 1999,
The Dee from the Cairngorms – Folklore and History from the Glens of Royal Deeside,
(Ballater: Lochnagar Publishing & Marketing).

Smith, R., 2004, *The Road to Maggieknockater*, (Edinburgh: Birlinn).

Whiteley, A. W. M., ed., 1998, *The Book of Bennachie*, 5th edn,
(Scotland: The Bailies of Bennachie).

Wyness, F., 1968, *Royal Valley*, (Aberdeen: Reid & Son).

Michael Pegler

Copyright

The Cairngorms, birthplace of the Dee © Bill Anderson
Braeriach, Cairngorms © Andrew Scott-Martin
King Edward VII Statue, Aberdeen © David Gowans/Alamy
John Brown © Mary Evans Picture Library
The Hunting Party © 2D Alan King/Alamy
The Queen's View © David Robertson/Alamy
Queen Victoria and John Brown at Balmoral Castle © Mary Evans Picture Library
Balmoral Castle © BL Images Limited
Crathes Castle © BL Images Limited/Alamy
Corgarff Castle © David Robertson
Old Bridge of Dee, Invercauld © Bill Anderson
Slow Walk © Fran Marquis-Faulkes
Cambus o' May Suspension Bridge © William Hume/Alamy
A feast near the source of the Dee © Bill Anderson
Water of Feugh, Banchory © Rule of Thirds/Alamy
A youthful Don © Norman Thomson
Stag © John Morgan
Hunting trip © Ricky Thomas
Fishing on the river © Terry Fincher
Lonach Gathering, Donside © Bill Anderson
Ballater © David Gowans
Deeside Moment I © Di Bumpus
Dawn over Deeside © Patricia Walter
Linn of Dee, Inverey © Scottish Viewpoint/Alamy
Sunset over Bennachie © Ray Liversidge
'Bennachie' © Norman Thomson
From the Bridge: Summer © Clare McCarthy
Autumn Cogs © Ricky Thomas
Paper Mill 1 © Rosemary Taylor
Fire Tree © Clare McCarthy

Ode to Craigievar Castle; The Waukrife Rogue; Lonach Hall; Reflections on the River Don from Towie Church © Lorna Alexander

Midmar Stone Circle and Balblair the Outlier; Waterfall; Estuary © Gerard Rochford

Heritage Trail; Portrait of a Fort; Turbulent Tributary; Ten Thousand Years of Life in the Garioch; The Last Fight; The Corgarff Brew; Tornahaish John © Norman G Thomson

The Native © Grisleda McGregor

A Deeside Summer © Catriona Yule

Dee journey; The Bonnie Banks o Dee; The Salmon; Ballater Bairnhood; Brig o Balgownie 1; Brig o Balgownie 2 © Sheena Blackhall

Twixt Dee and Don; Men O Lonach; Mither Dee; Spring in the Dee Valley © Mary Munro

Pines; Source; Just to hear your voice again; River Dee from the Old Invercauld Bridge; The Storm © Brian Lawrie

Dee Frost; Ice Dance on the Dee © Isabel Archibald

Granite's Child © Richard L Anderson

Far the Corbie Rins © Valerie Irvine-Fortescue

Postcard © Douglas W Gray

The Hunted; The Island © Martha Bottrell

Swans on the Lower Dee © Moira Brown

Song of the morn © Grace Banks

The River Don © Peter Banks

The Dee © Josh Banks

River Crossing © Fran Marquis-Faulkes

The Aberdeen Ferry Boat Disaster © Ann Nicol

About the Author

I was born in North Yorkshire and raised in South Devon, leaving home at sixteen to serve an engineering apprenticeship in the steel foundries of the West Midlands. I was subsequently employed as a draughtsman in the same industry before working as a cartographer with the M.O.D. Eventually I became interested in art and design. By 1978 I had become a glyptic sculptor. My work ranged in scale from small hand held pieces to monumental carvings. During the early years of my development I undertook various tasks in education, as a part-time teacher, adult tutor, and college lecturer. Along the way I was taught the discipline of writing analytic philosophy and I have engaged in research within that area whenever the opportunity presented itself.

Both my artistic and philosophical interest concerns the co-originality of private perception and public language. The latter is broadly concerned with tracing immanent connections that result in logically exchangeable patterns. Therefore, I was fascinated by the prospect of drawing attention to the host of interdependent themes that constitute this project. My task has been to contextualise the background details of each chapter. This content was gleaned from the work of other authors and from interviews with people who were familiar with the region.

MICHAEL PEGLER